Guide to America's Historical Geography
to accompany
Liberty, Equality, Power
A History of the American People
Second Edition

Volume I: To 1877

John M. Murrin
Paul E. Johnson
James M. McPherson
Gary Gerstle
Emily S. Rosenberg
Norman L. Rosenberg

Prepared by
Timothy J. McMannon

Harcourt Brace College Publishers

Fort Worth   Philadelphia   San Diego   New York   Orlando   Austin   San Antonio
Toronto   Montreal   London   Sydney   Tokyo

Cover Image: Albert Bierstadt, "The Oregon Trail," 1869. The Butler Institute of American Art, Youngstown, Ohio.

ISBN: 0-15-508109-8

Requests for permission to make copies of any part of the work should be mailed to:
Permissions Department, Harcourt Brace & Company, 6277 Sea Harbor Drive, Orlando, FL 32887-6777

Address for Editorial Correspondence:
Harcourt Brace College Publishers, 301 Commerce Street, Suite 3700, Fort Worth, TX 76102

Address for Orders:
Harcourt Brace & Company, 6277 Sea Harbor Drive, Orlando, FL 32887-6777. 1-800-782-4479

Web site address: http://www.hbcollege.com

Harcourt Brace College Publishers may provide complimentary instructional aids and supplements or supplement packages to those adopters qualified under our adoption policy. Please contact your sales representative for more information. If as an adopter or potential user you receive supplements you do not need, please return them to your sales representative or send them to:

Attention: Returns Department, Troy Warehouse, 465 South Lincoln Drive, Troy, MO 63379

Printed in the United States of America
8 9 0 1 2 3 4 5 6 7   202   10 9 8 7 6 5 4 3 2 1

Preface

This mapping workbook exposes students to the geography associated with American history. Using map exercises to complement the reading and study of textbook material can enliven that material and make it much more meaningful. It may enhance students' writing and analytical skills as well as heighten their appreciation for history as a discipline. The exercises in the *Guide to America's Historical Geography* have been prepared with these objectives in mind.

Each chapter of the workbook corresponds to a chapter of *Liberty, Equality, Power: A History of the American People*, Second Edition, and is divided into three sections: Map Exercises, Relating Maps and Text, and Essay Questions. The Map Exercises ask students to locate and label cities, bodies of water, states, battles, and other specific points included in the text's maps. In the Relating Maps and Text section, a fill-in-the-blank format allows students to test their knowledge of details found in *Liberty, Equality, Power: A History of the American People*, Second Edition. The Essay Questions require students to write short answers to several questions or to write a brief essay on a particular topic. Most of these questions ask students to incorporate the text's themes of liberty, equality, and power.

The information required to answer the questions in this workbook can be found through a careful reading of *Liberty, Equality, Power: A History of the American People*, Second Edition, and an examination of the suggested map references provided at the beginning of each workbook chapter. The Answer Key, located in the back of the workbook, includes completed maps, fill-in-the-blank answers, and brief sketches of suggested essay answers.

This revision of the workbook owes a great deal to the contributions of Charles A. Dranguet, Jr., and Victoria Reynolds Dranguet, preparers of the first edition.

Timothy J. McMannon

Contents

Chapter 1
When Old Worlds Collide: Contact, Conquest, Catastrophe

Chapter Summary

The story of America began millennia before the Spanish crown laid claim to land in the Western Hemisphere. It is theorized that three nomadic groups in five distinct waves ventured to these shores before Christopher Columbus's fateful voyage: Asians, Polynesians, and Norsemen. The most significant migration of the three was that of the Asians. These early people crossed Beringia, the land bridge between Asia and modern Alaska, perhaps as early as 50,000 years ago and again beginning about 23,000 B.C., during the most recent Ice Age. Descendants of the first travelers moved south and east, developing permanent settlements as they migrated. They reached Tierra del Fuego by 8000 B.C. Evidence of Polynesian contact with the Americas is circumstantial but significant: the presence of South American sweet potatoes on Easter Island. Just after A.D. 1000, Norsemen sailed from Greenland to a place they called Vinland (modern Newfoundland), but they soon retreated.

By the 1400s Europeans seeking an all-water route to the East began an age of exploration and expansion. Major navigational innovations enabled the small, peaceful country of Portugal to lead the way. Under Prince Henry ("the Navigator"), Portugal developed an excellent maritime educational system, extensively explored the African coast, instituted the slave trade, and began colonization. The maritime leadership of Vasco da Gama enabled Portuguese exploration to extend as far east as Japan and the Spice Islands. However, Portugal's South American colony, Brazil, would become the focal point of later Portuguese colonization efforts.

After Spain was politically united during the reigns of Ferdinand and Isabella, it joined Portugal in the exploration and colonization race. Columbus's successful voyage opened a new world to the Europeans. Magellan's circumnavigation of the earth finally proved that Columbus had, indeed, discovered a continent previously unknown to Europeans. Efforts by men such as Cortés assured conquest of the native population and acquisition of the wealth of these new lands for Spain.

When the Spanish entered Central and South America, they came into contact with complex, Stone-Age Mesoamerican and Andean cultures. These peoples, descendants of the Asians who had crossed Beringia during the Ice Ages, had begun to establish sedentary cultures after about 4000 B.C., when some began practicing agriculture. Other groups remained nomadic. The most powerful and wealthy of these peoples lived in the Valley of Mexico and in the Andes.

The meeting of peoples from Europe and the Americas inevitably resulted in conflict, for the cultures differed dramatically in religion, warfare objectives, and social organization.

Ultimately, the Spanish *conquistadores* subjugated the most powerful empires of Central and South America. Not satisfied with the wealth they found there, the Spanish also entered the interior of North America, searching unsuccessfully for fabled cities of gold.

European diseases devastated the Native Americans. Many who did not succumb to disease were enslaved in the *encomienda* system. By the end of the 1500s, Spain had conquered the Americas, but she would be challenged for control of this vast region.

Map References

The exercises and questions in this chapter relate to the text of Chapter 1 of *Liberty, Equality, Power: A History of the American People* and the following maps.

Map Exercises

1. Label the following on Map 1-A:
   a. Beringia
   b. Greenland
   c. Meadowcroft site
   d. Aleutian Islands
   e. Iceland

2. Locate and label the following on Map 1-A:
   a. Hispaniola
   b. Cuba
   c. Jamaica
   d. Vera Cruz
   e. Mexico City (Tenochtitlán)
   f. Yucatán Peninsula
   g. Puerto Rico
   h. Bahama Islands
   i. Chichén Itzá
   j. Caribbean Sea
   k. Gulf of Mexico

3. Locate with a dot and label the following cities on Map 1-B:
   a. Constantinople
   b. Naples
   c. Baghdad
   d. Palos
   e. Genoa

Map 1-A: North America and the Caribbean

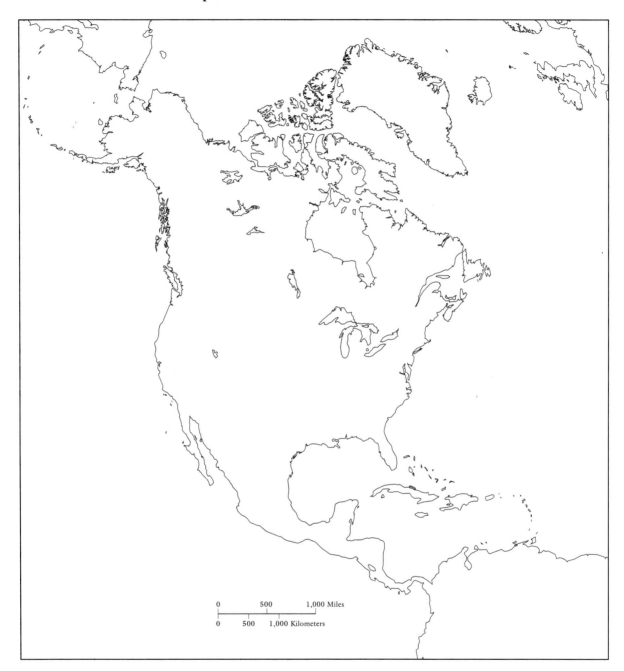

Map 1-B: Africa and the Mediterranean in the 15th Century

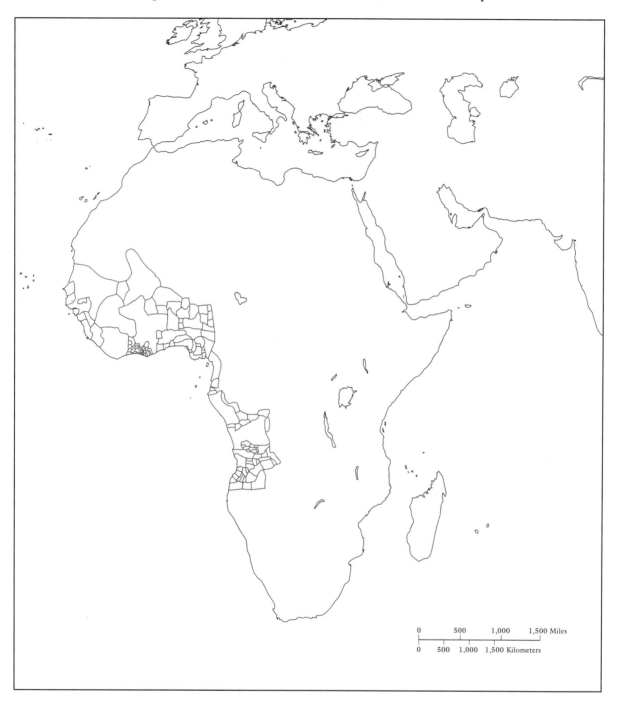

4. Locate and label the following bodies of water on Map 1-B:
   a. Mediterranean Sea
   b. Atlantic Ocean
   c. Indian Ocean

5. Locate and label the following on Map 1-B:
   a. Portugal
   b. Castile
   c. Empire of Mali
   d. Cape Bojador
   e. Madeira Islands
   f. Azores
   g. Cape Verde Islands
   h. Arguin Island
   i. Kingdom of the Kongo
   j. Benin
   k. Cape of Good Hope
   l. Rhodes
   m. Cyprus
   n. Malta
   o. Crete
   p. Canary Islands
   q. Sahara
   r. Arabia

Relating Maps and Text

1. During the Ice Ages, a land bridge geographers call _____ appeared between Asia and North America.

2. Mesoamerica includes _____ and southern and central _____.

3. In A.D. 982–983, _____ led the Norsemen to _____. In A.D. 1001 his son _____ began to explore the coast of North America, where he founded a colony called _____. Although the Norse abandoned this settlement, they continued to return to the area for a century, most likely to get _____.

4. Before A.D. 1460, the Portuguese founded island colonies off the coasts of Portugal and Africa including the _____, _____, and the _____ island groups. In 1487 _____ was the first European to round the Cape of Good Hope; ten years later _____ sailed to India.

5. During the early 15th century, Spain sent settlers to the _____, but did little other exploring or colonizing. The 1469 marriage of Ferdinand of _____ and Isabella of _____ would lead to the creation of modern Spain.

6. Name the European explorer

    a. who searched Florida for the fountain of youth. _____

    b. who became the first European to reach the Pacific Ocean. _____

    c. whose fleet sailed around the world, 1519–1522. _____

    d. who conquered the Aztec of Mexico._____

    e. who conquered the Inca of Peru. _____

    f. who traveled into New Mexico, Arizona, Texas and Kansas. _____

7. The largest city north of Mexico from A.D. 900 to 1250 was _____. In what is now the southwestern United States the _____ developed an extensive irrigation system and the _____ were noted astronomers.

8. In 1492 at least _____ million people lived in the Americas.

Essay Question

1. The old worlds of Europe and the Americas collided in 1492. Why was it impossible for the two worlds to coexist peacefully after that collision?

Chapter 2

The Challenge to Spain and the Settlement of North America

Chapter Summary

In 1517, while Spain was claiming and conquering much of the Americas, Martin Luther inadvertently initiated the Protestant Reformation in Europe. The birth of the Lutheran and Calvinist faiths not only led to bloodshed and migrations within Europe, it also shaped colonization in the Americas. By 1600, Catholic Spain's dominance in North America faced serious challenges from France, the Netherlands, and England, all three of which had powerful Protestant movements.

France's challenge to Spain's control of North America began as early as 1524; however, a successful French settlement was not established until the early 17th century. While both Catholics and Huguenots (Protestants) originally explored and settled in the St. Lawrence River valley in New France, Catholicism ultimately became the official religion of that area. Early French colonial efforts centered on converting the Indians and establishing a fur trade with them. The French Jesuits mastered the native languages, lived among the Indians, and converted thousands of them, while the *coureurs de bois* established the French fur trade.

The French impact, however, was greatest in the Caribbean, where very lucrative sugar plantations were established. To provide labor for the plantations, the French enslaved the native population, setting the stage for later troubles.

The Dutch impact upon North America was also substantial. They established ideas of religious tolerance, commercial prosperity, and personal freedom in their American colonies. However, the major motivation for Dutch expansion was economic profit and not settlement.

England's first attempt at settlement in the New World was on Roanoke Island. It failed, with the settlers disappearing under mysterious circumstances. Not long after England successfully waged war against Spain, however, the British established their first permanent settlement, Jamestown, in 1607. After years of near–devastation, the colony of Virginia finally became successful, mostly because of its production and exportation of tobacco. The headright system and indentured servitude provided the labor. In 1619, the first Africans arrived in Jamestown as indentured servants. However, by the end of the 1600s, slavery was firmly established in the Chesapeake colonies, and a racial caste system was rigidly in place.

The second Chesapeake colony, Maryland, was initially established to provide religious freedom for Catholics. Ironically, religious tolerance by the Catholics caused their control to be short–lived.

The New England colonies were settled primarily by religious dissenters such as the Calvinist–oriented Pilgrims and Puritans, and these colonies were heavily influenced by their religious ideologies. However, the world's first bill of rights was issued in this region, and the idea of equality among the heads of households was initiated here.

During the 17th century, while England was greatly extending its empire, it faced internal problems that ultimately influenced its extensive colonial holdings. In the 1640s, England experienced political upheaval, including civil war and revolution. During the difficult times, the mother country devoted little attention to her possessions.

During the Restoration Era (1660–1688), England founded or took possession of the colonies of North and South Carolina, New York, East and West New Jersey, and Pennsylvania. All of them were proprietary, and each offered guarantees of political and civil liberties, as well as religious toleration, to attract settlers.

Map References

The exercises and questions in this chapter relate to the following maps and corresponding text in Chapter 2 of *Liberty, Equality, Power: A History of the American People*.

New France and the Jesuit Missions (p. 49)

Roanoke Colony, 1584–1590 (p. 55)

Virginia and Maryland, circa 1675 (p. 62)

New England in the 1640s (p. 68)

The Duke of York's Colonial Charter (p. 78)

Early Pennsylvania and New Jersey, circa 1700 (p. 83)

Map Exercises

1. Label the following on Map 2:
    a. Jamestown
    b. Plymouth
    c. Nova Scotia (Acadia)
    d. New Amsterdam (New York City)
    e. Quebec
    f. Three Rivers
    g. Montreal
    h. Ft. Orange (Albany)
    i. Roanoke Island
    j. Philadelphia

2. Label the location of the following Indian groups on Map 2:
    a. Algonquians
    b. Iroquois
    c. Hurons

3. Label the following rivers or bodies of water on Map 2:
    a. St. Lawrence River
    b. Delaware Bay
    c. Hudson River
    d. Connecticut River
    e. Chesapeake Bay
    f. Pamlico Sound

Map 2: Atlantic Coast of North America

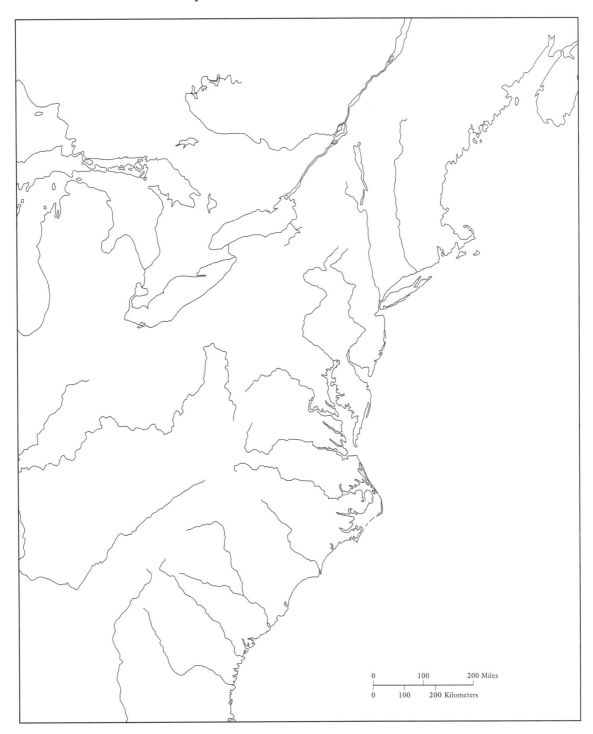

Harcourt Brace & Company

Relating Maps and Text

1. During the 16th and 17th centuries, French explorations and discoveries in North America included the following:

   a. the Verrazano expedition, which explored the Atlantic coast from the _____ to _____, noting the harbor potential of _____.

   b. the Cartier expedition, which explored the _____ River.

   c. the voyages of Samuel de Champlain, which established the Huguenot settlement in _____ and also founded _____ in 1608.

2. In 1626, the Dutch purchased _____ from the Indians and founded the port of _____. They also established _____ about 150 miles upriver to trade with the _____ Indians.

3. During the 16th century, England sent several expeditions to the new world. They included:

   a. the voyage of _____, an Italian navigator, who searched for a northwest passage to Asia and possibly reached _____.

   b. the voyage of _____, who rounded Cape Horn and raided Spanish territory along the Pacific coast of Peru, sailed west, and completed the first _____ since Magellan's crew's.

   c. two unsuccessful attempts to plant colonies off present-day North Carolina on _____ by _____, which ended British attempts at North American settlement before 1600.

4. Under the auspices of the _____, the settlement of _____ was established in 1607 on the James River. The colony owed its physical survival to _____ who forced the colonists to raise grain. The colony's economic survival is attributed to _____, who introduced _____ as a cash crop.

5. The colony of _____ was founded as a haven for English Catholics.

6. By the mid-17th century, _____ became the main cash crop in the English settlements in the West Indies.

7. The _____ landed in Plymouth; the _____ settled the Massachusetts Bay colony. These New Englanders soon began exporting _____ and _____ to other colonies.

8. Some New England colonies were founded by religious dissenters. They included Rhode Island, founded by _____ and _____, and _____, founded by Thomas Hooker.

9. By the early 1700s, _____ became the chief export of South Carolina and encouraged the massive growth of _____ in the colony.

10. In 1664 James, Duke of York, seized the Dutch colony of _____ and renamed it _____. Nine years later, the Dutch temporarily retook the city of _____ and renamed it _____.

11. The Quakers founded the colonies of _____ and _____. The latter colony became economically successful in its trade with the Caribbean as an exporter of _____ and _____.

Essay Question

1. European settlement in the New World brought the newcomers into contact with the indigenous Indian populations. Compare and contrast the relationships of the colonies of France, the Netherlands, Spain, and England with the Indians.

Chapter 3
England Discovers Its Colonies: Empire, Liberty, and Expansion

Chapter Summary

During the difficult times of the 1640s, England devoted little attention to her possessions in North America and the Caribbean. By the 1650s, however, England rediscovered the colonies.

While the British colonies had many common traits, they developed different demographic, racial, and religious mixes and different forms of government. Beginning in the Caribbean and moving northward, the colonies became more economically diverse and less based on a slave economy, less ethnically diverse, less Anglican but more pious, more literate, healthier, and more balanced in terms of the sexes. Offsetting these differences, however, were their common language, legal system, and heritage: commonalities that would ultimately unite them as a nation.

Throughout most of Europe, nations recognized the importance of embracing mercantilism to achieve and maintain power. Following this form of economic policy, England greatly altered the role of legislation regarding its colonial possessions. Parliament passed the first Navigation Act in 1651 to address Dutch economic competition. In the 1660s and 1670s, additional legislation was enacted to establish English hegemony over all Atlantic trade, although England did not immediately enforce these trade acts.

It became evident after 1670 that colonial migration to the West was inevitable. The Indian population posed a serious but temporary block to this expansion. In 1675, war broke out between the Wampanoag Indians, led by Metacom (or King Philip, as the English called him) and English settlers in the Plymouth colony. Soon, Connecticut and Massachusetts joined the war, turning against nearby Narragansetts. That same year, Virginia colonists battled the Doeg and Susquehannock Indians. As in Latin America, Indian–European interactions had serious negative consequences for the Indians. Warfare, European diseases, religious conversions, new commodities, and new technologies challenged the eastern Indians' way of life and ultimately resulted in their demise.

Bacon's Rebellion in Virginia in 1676 proved to be the largest social upheaval in the American colonies before the Revolution. Arising from a disagreement over the correct strategy to use against frontier Indians, the rebellion pitted frontier settlers against tidewater planters. Colonists attacked the Indians and other colonists. Eventually, the royal government collapsed. This conflict helped to bring about a political crisis in England in the 1670s and 1680s which, in turn, affected the colonies. First, the Lords of Trade were created to enforce the Navigation Acts and to administer the colonies. Then, the Crown attempted to consolidate the New England colonies by establishing the centralized Dominion of New England. However, the Glorious Revolution in 1688 put an end to the rule of James and the much-resented Dominion. By the end of the 17th century, Puritan dominance in New England and political upheaval in England had likewise ended.

From 1689 on, the British government claimed total power over the colonies. By 1720 all but two of the colonies had come under royal control. In practice, however, that control was not absolute. The Glorious Revolution guaranteed representative government for England and her colonies. England's new constitution guaranteed that the government's power would be controlled by the people, thus ensuring liberty and the right to property.

The colonial empires—England, France and Spain—developed in isolation from one another, but by the end of the seventeenth century, they were drawn into conflict by intense warfare in Europe.

From 1689 to 1716, the French and English engaged in mortal combat at home and abroad. When peace returned, France and England resumed their expansion.

Map References

The exercises and questions in this chapter relate to the following maps and corresponding text in Chapter 3 of *Liberty, Equality, Power: A History of the American People.*

       Area of English Settlement by 1700 (p. 88)

       New England in Metacom's War, 1675–1676 (p. 100)

       Government and Religion in the British Colonies, 1720 (p. 111)

       French Middle Ground, circa 1700 (p. 117)

       Southeastern Theater of War, 1702–1713 (p. 121)

Map Exercises

1. Locate and label the following colonies on Map 3:
   a. New York
   b. New Jersey
   c. Pennsylvania
   d. North Carolina
   e. South Carolina
   f. Connecticut
   g. Massachusetts
   h. New Hampshire
   i. Rhode Island
   j. Delaware
   k. Virginia

2. Locate and label the following on Map 3:
   a. Martha's Vineyard
   b. Nantucket
   c. New France

3. Locate with a dot and label the following cities on Map 3:
   a. Boston
   b. St. Augustine
   c. Charles Town (Charleston)
   d. New York City

Map 3: British Colonies, circa 1720

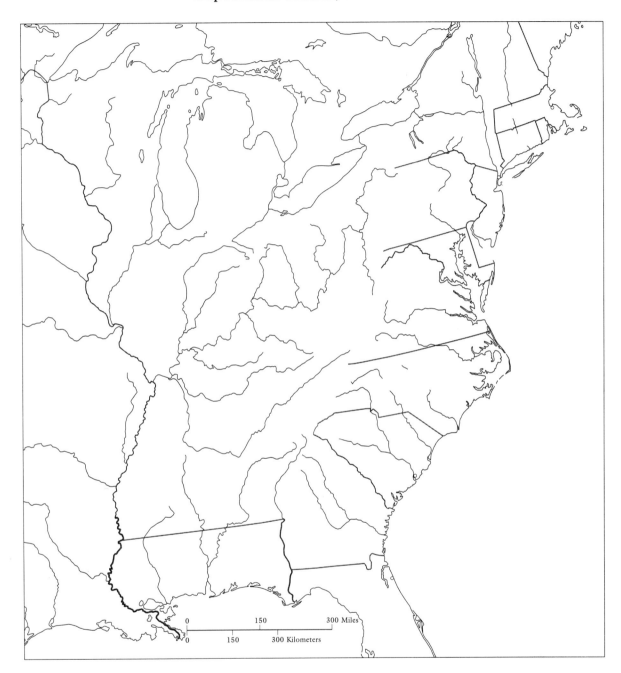

Relating Maps and Text

1. In the 1640s, while the English were embroiled in civil war, the _____ seized control of trade with England's _____ and _____ colonies. By 1650 most sugar and tobacco exports were going to _____ rather than London. Parliament passed the first of a series of _____ in 1651 to regain hegemony over Atlantic trade.

2. New England Protestants began serious efforts to convert the Indians in the 1640s on the island of _____ and in the Indian town of _____, near Roxbury, Massachusetts.

3. During Bacon's Rebellion in 1676, friendly _____ Indians and unresisting _____ Indians were massacred by _____ men. The city of _____ was burned to the ground.

4. In 1686, King James II sent the former governor of New York, _____ to govern the newly created _____ in _____. Soon the king added the colonies of _____, _____, _____, _____, _____, and both Jerseys.

5. In 1707 _____ and _____ merged their parliaments and became the single kingdom of _____.

6. The most successful Indian revolt in American history took place in 1680 at _____ in the Spanish province of _____.

7. The region around the Great Lakes became a _____ over which no one wielded complete power, although _____ had great influence there.

Essay Question

1. From a geographical and economic standpoint, why would merchants in New York City in the 1680s find resettlement in Pennsylvania attractive?

Chapter 4

Provincial America and the Struggle for a Continent

Chapter Summary

By the beginning of the 18th century, distinct regions solidified in England's colonies. The southernmost region was characterized by plantations and slavery, giving rise to the "Old South." The Middle Atlantic region was highly pluralistic, with immigrants from Ireland, Germany, and Wales. This prosperous region became North America's breadbasket. The New England region supported maritime occupations, farming, and trade, but its economy and population were declining compared to those of the other regions.

Despite regional differences, the American colonies were all becoming increasingly Anglicized, as Americans built English-style houses, imported goods from England, and adopted British patterns of social and gender relationships. The Enlightenment, emphasizing science, reason, and human capacities, made its way from England to the colonies. The Great Awakening, a religious movement embracing emotional revivalism and individual conversion, had roots on both sides of the Atlantic and gave birth in the colonies to new Protestant denominations and colleges.

By the mid-1700s, the British colonists were very content with their lives. They owned property, had a voice in their local government, and thought they enjoyed the ultimate in liberty. By 1720, all but two of the colonies had an appointed governor, a council, and an elected assembly. Almost three-fourths of all free adult white males could vote, and all of the colonies had constitutions.

The major powers of Europe again engaged in continual warfare from 1739 to 1763. Numerous military conflicts took place in North America as well, from the Caribbean in the south to New France in the north. In 1754, the greatest of the colonial wars began between France and England. At stake was ultimate control of North America. The French and Indian War began as the result of a clash between New France and Virginia; each laid claim to the same land in the Ohio River valley. During this war, the British colonists attempted colonial unity for the first time. At the Albany Conference in New York in 1754, the unification plan was presented but failed to obtain colonial approval or support. London also rejected the colonial plan for defense, fearing that a dangerous precedent might be set.

The conflict soon spread to Europe and became a world war. Virtually unnoticed by the contending Europeans was a shift in Indian tribes' relationships with each other. During the war, they began to exhibit a pan-Indian unity, carefully trying to avoid conflict with each other despite alliances that put them on opposite sides. Afterwards, they would not accept the treaty provisions. After England reorganized its government and named William Pitt as war minister, an English victory was assured. Spain, which had remained neutral for most of the war, entered the conflict in 1762 on the side of France but was too late to influence the outcome. In 1763, the Peace of Paris was signed and the war ended. Huge tracts of land changed hands: France ceded to Britain all of North America east of the Mississippi River (except New Orleans, which went to Spain), Spain gained possession of French territory west of the Mississippi, and Britain secured Florida from the Spanish. England was victorious and the colonists were ecstatic. In twelve short years, however, England's vast new empire would crumble.

Map References

The exercises and questions in this chapter relate to the following maps and corresponding text in Chapter 4 of *Liberty, Equality, Power: A History of the American People.*

> France versus Britain in North America by 1755 (p. 154)
>
> British Offensives, 1755 (p. 156)
>
> Conquest of Canada, 1758–1760 (p. 161)
>
> Growth of Population to 1760 (p. 162)

Map Exercises

1. Label the following cities on Map 4:
    a. Albany
    b. Schenectady
    c. Québec
    d. Montréal
    e. Boston

2. Label the following bodies of water on Map 4:
    a. all five Great Lakes
    b. Lake Champlain
    c. Lake George

3. Locate with a dot and label the following forts on Map 4. Indicate with "B" those forts built by Britain; "F" those built by France.
    a. Louisbourg
    b. St. Frederic (Crown Point)
    c. Frontenac
    d. Port Royal
    e. Halifax
    f. Detroit
    g. Oswego
    h. Beauséjour
    i. Carillon (Ticonderoga)
    j. Duquesne
    k. Presque Isle
    l. Niagara
    m. William Henry
    n. Edward

Map 4: Northeast during the French and Indian War

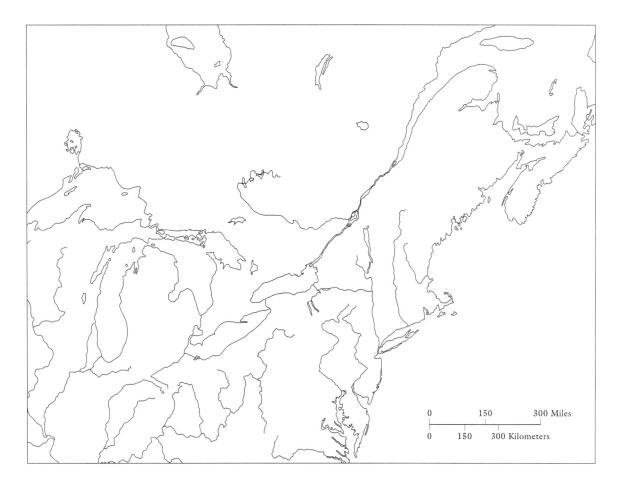

0   150   300 Miles

0   150   300 Kilometers

Relating Maps and Text

1. Slaves who labored on the tobacco plantations in the _____ colonies were worked in groups known as _____. About _____ percent of slaves in that region were skilled artisans. _____ became a second cash crop there, and its cultivation and exportation prompted the rise of cities such as _____ and _____ and the expansion of the _____ industry.

2. In the _____ rice fields, the labor system was known as the _____ system. By the middle of the 18th century, _____, used as a dye in the British _____ industry, had become a second staple crop in that region.

3. By 1770, only Virginia had a greater population than _____; by 1775 the city of _____ was the largest in British North America. In _____, on the other hand, more people were leaving than arriving after about 1660.

4. _____ invented fiat currency in 1690 but converted to silver currency in 1750, with disastrous results.

5. In the first half of the eighteenth century, the city of _____ was the printing capital of North America. John Peter Zenger, publisher of the _____ was acquitted of a charge of seditious libel in 1735 and thus advanced freedom of the press in the colonies.

6. The founders of utopian _____, centered on the city of _____, envisioned a colony of armed freemen, producing _____ and _____ with no _____ or _____.

7. Revivals during the Great Awakening destroyed the unity of the _____ Church in New England, increased previously low levels of denominationalism in the _____ colonies, and broke down localism by creating new links with _____.

8. Spanish _____ offered freedom to any slave who escaped from British colonies and converted to Catholicism. In 1738 a new town, _____, was established and became the first community of free blacks in what is now the United States.

9. The French constructed military posts from Fort _____ to Fort _____ to stop British settlement west of the _____.

10. After Braddock's defeat in 1755, the colony of _____ faced frontier war for the first time.

11. In Europe during the Seven Years' War, _____, _____, and _____ fought against _____, which was aided by _____. For most of the war, _____ remained neutral.

Essay Question

1. Describe several developments between 1700 and 1760 that advanced ideas of equality in the British North American colonies. Describe several developments that furthered inequality.

Harcourt Brace & Company

Chapter 5
Reform, Resistance, Revolution

Chapter Summary

After the Seven Years' War ended, Prime Minister George Grenville decided that the American colonists should help pay for their own defense. The government issued the Proclamation Act of 1763 and a series of acts designed to halt smuggling and to centralize the government's control of the colonies. These actions irreparably damaged the relationship between the mother country and her colonial possessions; colonists from New Hampshire to Georgia united as never before in protest against what they perceived to be a usurpation of their British rights and liberties. Eventually, they would unite in revolution.

From 1765 to 1775, three major crises ultimately destroyed Britain's North American empire: the Stamp Act crisis, the events surrounding the Townshend Revenue Act, and the incidents that occurred in response to the Tea Act. These three crises brought on a war that neither side wanted or expected but that both sides made inevitable.

The first imperial crisis stemmed from the Stamp Act of 1765. When Parliament passed the act over the vocal objections of colonists and a number of members of Parliament, it considered its actions in line with previous imperial measures. The colonists felt differently, believing that the Stamp Act was an attempt to raise revenue, not to regulate trade. Interpreted in that way, it was an unconstitutional attempt by Parliament to confiscate colonists' property; taxation was something only the colonial assemblies could undertake. Through coordinated action and the vigilante activism of the "Sons of Liberty," the colonies (save Georgia) managed to keep stamped paper from ever being circulated. Although Parliament issued a Declaratory Act stating its authority over the colonies, it repealed the loathsome and unenforceable Stamp Act. The colonists jubilantly celebrated their victory.

In 1767, smarting from the Stamp Act rebuke, many members of Parliament eagerly welcomed Charles Townshend's plan to impose taxes on the recalcitrant colonists. Townshend argued that the colonies would agree to duties on tea, lead, glass, and other enumerated imports. Townshend could not have been more in error, and the result of his miscalculation was the second major crisis of the period. Rejecting Townshend's distinction between internal and external taxation, the colonists again organized resistance to Parliamentary actions, this time through non-importation agreements, by which colonial merchants would not import British goods. Once again, Parliament eventually backed down, averting a prolonged crisis by repealing all of the Townshend duties except the one on tea.

The third and final crisis stemmed from another fateful act of Parliament, the 1773 Tea Act. This legislation was designed to induce the colonists to buy duted tea and thus save the East India Company, which was losing business to smugglers of Dutch tea. In response, Boston's Sons of Liberty threw several shiploads of East India Company tea into Boston Harbor. The ensuing reaction of Parliament, the Coercive Acts, precipitated concerted colonial action, including the First Continental Congress, which took the first steps toward independence. By April 1775, the colonists and the British empire were at war.

The same misunderstandings, fears, and lack of trust that had led to the imperial crises and the Boston Massacre proved too deep-seated to repair by negotiation. Neither the Olive Branch Petition nor any other attempts at reconciliation could stem the growing movement toward American independence. By July 2, 1776, the colonies had rejected all Parliamentary authority and, with the help of Thomas Paine's radical pamphlet *Common Sense*, severed their ties to the British monarchy. When the Continental Congress adopted the Declaration of Independence on July 4, the United States came into being—at least on parchment.

Map References

The exercises and questions in this chapter relate to the following maps and the text in Chapter 5 of *Liberty, Equality, Power: A History of the American People.*

> Growth of Population to 1760 (p. 162)
>
> Pontiac's War and the Proclamation Line of 1763 (p. 170)
>
> Feudal Revival: Great Estates of Late Colonial America (p. 187)
>
> Lexington, Concord, and Boston, 1775–1776 (p. 197)

Map Exercises

1. Label the following cities on Map 5:
   a. Boston
   b. Newport
   c. New York City
   d. Philadelphia
   e. Charleston, SC
   f. Providence, RI
   g. Falmouth (Portland)
   h. Concord, MA
   i. Lexington

2. Shade in and label the following land grant areas on Map 5:
   a. Fairfax Estate
   b. Granville District
   c. Livingston Manor
   d. Rensselaerswyck Manor

3. Label the following on Map 5:
   a. Indian Reserve
   b. Spanish Louisiana
   c. Georgia

4. Draw in and label the Proclamation Line of 1763 on Map 5.

Relating Maps and Text

1. Following the Seven Years' War, Britain gave back to France the islands of _____ and _____. The British might have turned over _____, had France asked for it.

2. Britain's _____ established a line along the _____ watershed, beyond which English settlers were not to go.

Map 5: Late Colonial America

3. In a 1763 conflict known as _____, several Indian nations united to try to drive British troops from posts in the West. In Pennsylvania, a group of Scots-Irish vigilantes known as the _____ attacked unarmed Christian Indians.

Harcourt Brace & Company

4. In October 1765, the Stamp Act Congress met in _____. Because of widespread resistance to the Stamp Act, stamp masters in every colony but _____ resigned before the law took effect. The cities of _____ and _____ had the highest levels of violence in response to the Act.

5. The colony of _____ refused to accept the Quartering Act, leading Parliament to pass the _____.

6. After a British customs vessel, the *Gaspée*, ran aground near _____, men in disguise wounded the captain and burned the ship.

7. Lord North expected that the Coercive Acts would isolate the city of _____ from the province of _____ and the province from the rest of _____.

8. When General Gage called for a General Court to meet in _____, many Massachusetts towns chose instead to send delegates to a provincial congress in _____.

9. On July 2, 1776, when the Second Continental Congress voted for independence, British troops began landing on _____ to put down the rebellion.

Essay Question

1. In Britain's North American colonies before 1765, elected assemblies levied taxes and enjoyed the privilege of self–government. Thus, at least the semblance of political equality with the Parliament in London existed. Give several examples of the changes that occurred in Britain's policies toward her colonies after 1765 that deprived the colonists of their political equality.

Chapter 6
The Revolutionary Republic

Chapter Summary

Having declared their independence on July 4, 1776, the American colonies found themselves in a tremendous struggle to make that independence a reality. The Revolutionary War was far longer and more costly than either the Americans or the British could have predicted in 1776. It began badly for the colonists: the Americans were pushed back from Quebec and lost Long Island, New York City, and most of New Jersey. Only Washington's daring victories at Trenton and Princeton in December 1776 and January 1777 salvaged the campaign and gave Americans hope that the Revolution could survive.

Encouraged by the American victory at Saratoga in 1777, but at the same time concerned that the fall of Philadelphia would push the Americans to surrender, the French government formed an alliance with the United States at the beginning of 1778 and entered the war. In 1779 Spain also declared war on the British Empire. During 1780, the British took the fight to the southern colonies, capturing Charleston and moving almost at will through the Carolinas. But finally, by October 1781, combined French and American forces surrounded Lord Cornwallis's army of eight thousand men at Yorktown, Virginia, and forced their surrender. Lord North's government resigned in early 1782, bringing in a new ministry committed to peace in America. In 1783, the British recognized American independence by signing the Treaty of Paris. The Revolutionary War was over.

By the terms of the Treaty of Paris of 1783, the borders of the United States extended from the Mississippi River eastward to the Atlantic Ocean and from Spanish Florida northward to British Canada.

The War for Independence had been as much a civil war as a revolution. About one-sixth of the white population of the colonies remained loyal to Britain and, when given a choice, most slaves south of New England and most Indians supported the British. Tens of thousands of refugees left the colonies for other parts of the empire, many moving to Canada. Women began to assert their own independence of men, challenging the traditionally patriarchal Anglo-American society.

The Articles of Confederation, drafted in 1776 and 1777, proved a rather ineffectual basis for government for the new republic. With several major deficiencies, particularly a lack of the power to tax, the Congress proved far too weak. The Congress did, however, pass the Northwest Ordinance of 1787, which provided for admitting new states as full equals of the original thirteen, outlawed slavery north of the Ohio River, and made provision for public education. Indians on the frontier, however, refused to accept that the United States extended to the Mississippi River, as the Treaty of Paris asserted, and white settlers found the Ohio River valley to be particularly dangerous.

Economic crisis, Shays's rebellion, and deteriorating foreign affairs opened the eyes of many Americans to the need to replace or amend the Articles of Confederation. In May 1787, the Constitutional Convention was called into session in Philadelphia. Members of the convention decided to scrap the Articles entirely. In the ensuing four months, they constructed an entirely new government with vastly increased powers and a system of checks and balances. The new Constitution granted sovereignty to the people who, in turn, entrusted the various levels of government with power. By creating separate and independent branches of government, by establishing a bicameral legislature, and by staggering elections, the Constitutional Convention created a remarkably resilient balance of liberty and power.

Map References

The exercises and questions in this chapter relate to the following maps and corresponding text in Chapter 6 of *Liberty, Equality, Power: A History of the American People.*

Revolutionary War in the Northern States (p. 207)

War in the Lower South, 1780-1781 (p. 222)

Virginia and the Yorktown Campaign (p. 227)

Map Exercises

1. Locate with a dot and label the following cities, forts, and battles on Map 6-A:

    a. Trenton

    b. Princeton

    c. Valley Forge

Map 6-A: Revolutionary War in the Northern States

    d.   Fort Ticonderoga

    e.   Saratoga

    f.   Brandywine

    g.   Monmouth Courthouse

2.   Locate with a dot and label the following cities and battles on Map 6-B:

    a.   Annapolis

    b.   Richmond

    c.   Yorktown

    d.   the Capes

    e.   Baltimore

Map 6-B: Virginia and the Yorktown Campaign

Relating Maps and Text

1. During the early months of the Revolutionary War, British forces captured the city of _____ to control both ends of _____ Sound.

2. In October 1777, British General John Burgoyne was forced to surrender at _____.

3. Spain entered the war against Great Britain in hopes of retaking _____. Although the Spanish failed to achieve that goal, they did capture _____, and the British ceded _____ after the war.

4. _____ was the first state to adopt a permanent, republican constitution. The oldest constitution in the world, however, is that of the state of _____.

5. By 1780 the British had turned their attention to the _____. The surrender of 5,000 colonials at _____ in May gave the British army its greatest number of prisoners. But Continental forces dealt loyalist troops a crushing defeat at _____ in October.

6. Continental soldiers from _____ mutinied on New Year's Day, 1781, and troops from _____ mutinied soon thereafter.

7. Both Cornwallis and Washington believed that events in _____ would decide the outcome of the war. They were right: Cornwallis surrendered at _____ in October 1781, breaking Britain's will to continue the war.

8. In 1780, the state of _____ instituted the first gradual emancipation statute. By 1800 the city of _____ had the largest population of free blacks in North America.

9. The Land Ordinance of 1785 provided for the survey and division of the Northwest Territory into townships _____ miles square with _____ sections of _____ acres.

10. When the Constitutional Convention assembled in the city of _____ in May 1787, only the state of _____ refused to send a delegation. The delegates from _____ suggested equal representation for all states in one house of the proposed Congress and proportional representation based on population in the other. This idea provided an opportunity for compromise between the _____ or "large state" plan and the plan offered by a delegate from _____ on behalf of the small states.

Essay Question

1. Perhaps the most revolutionary outcome of the American War for Independence was its geographical impact. What geographical changes resulted from the war?

Chapter 7
The Democratic Republic, 1790–1820

Chapter Summary

In 1790, the young United States extended from the Mississippi River eastward to the Atlantic Ocean and from Spanish Florida northward to British Canada. The majority of the population, however, lived near the Atlantic coast. The 1790 census revealed that only the five seaport cities of Boston, New York, Philadelphia, Baltimore, and Charleston had populations of over 10,000. The economy of these cities depended upon imports from Europe and American farm exports. By 1815, New York City had become America's most populated urban complex.

Despite growth in the cities, the United States was an overwhelmingly rural nation in 1790: 94 percent of the American population lived on farms. The farm also influenced American social values. Most people shared Thomas Jefferson's perception that farmers were "the chosen people of God." Land ownership gave one a stake in American society: property and liberty were considered to be inseparably linked. Many farm families supplemented their incomes through household industry.

By 1790, westward expansion in the United States was on the rise, as more white Americans sought farmland. Native Americans soon faced land and wildlife shortages, epidemics, and social and military clashes with whites. In 1794, after losing the Battle of Fallen Timbers, the Indians of the Old Northwest were forced to sign the Treaty of Greenville, by which they ceded a huge tract of land in what is now Ohio and Indiana. Most of the eastern woodlands Indians were subdued as a result of the 1811 Battle of Tippecanoe, in which William Henry Harrison's forces defeated Tecumseh's powerful Indian confederation, and the War of 1812, in which the Indian confederacy allied with the British.

Life in the backcountry was very difficult. Westerners asked only two things of the new American government: the right to navigate the Mississippi and Ohio Rivers and protection from the Indians. Within three decades, the western population grew from about 10,000 to over 2 million. By 1820, the western edge of the nation was no longer disparaged as the "backcountry" but rather perceived as the American frontier and the doorway to America's future.

By the end of the 1700s, slavery appeared to be dying. The Chesapeake area was growing less tobacco, thus requiring less labor. The farmers of Virginia and Delaware led the way in emancipating their slaves. However, in the South, cotton production was on the rise, and so was the need for a large, dependable labor force. In 1793, Eli Whitney invented the cotton gin and almost immediately cotton became "king." This labor-intensive crop rejuvenated slavery, and thus liberty and equality for most American black slaves was doomed. The plantation system spread from the Chesapeake to Virginia and Tennessee, then to Georgia, Alabama, and Mississippi.

Slavery became intertwined with another significant social development of the era: the growth of evangelical Protestant religion. The Baptist and Methodist faiths were the most successful of these new, democratic sects. In the 1780s, Methodist leaders called for slaves to be freed, but the increasing commitment to slavery in the South forced the Methodists to back away from that stance by the early 1800s.

Even though the United States had become a democratic nation, not everyone was represented in that democracy. Women, children, slaves, and Native Americans still lacked power; white property–holding males continued to control the nation.

Map References

The exercises and questions in this chapter relate to the text of Chapter 7 of *Liberty, Equality, Power: A History of the American People* and the following maps.

Native America, 1783–1812 (p. 251)
Securing the West, 1790–1796 (p. 285)

Map Exercises

1. Label the following states, cities, or territories on Map 7:
    a. Kentucky
    b. Tennessee
    c. Ohio
    d. Louisiana
    e. Indiana Territory
    f. Mississippi Territory
    g. Illinois Territory
    h. Missouri Territory

2. Locate the sites and give the dates of the following battles on Map 7:
    a. Fallen Timbers
    b. Tippecanoe

3. Label the locations of the following native American tribes on Map 7:
    a. Chickasaw
    b. Creek
    c. Cherokee
    d. Shawnee
    e. Winnebago
    f. Potawatomi
    g. Kickapoo
    h. Ottawa
    i. Wyandot

Relating Maps and Text

1. Because little specie circulated in the United States in 1790 and no paper money had yet been issued, Americans developed regional systems of exchange. In _____, farmers kept meticulous accounts of debts; in the _____ and _____, however, farmers used a _____ in which they remembered what they owed.

Harcourt Brace & Company

Map 7: The West, circa 1800

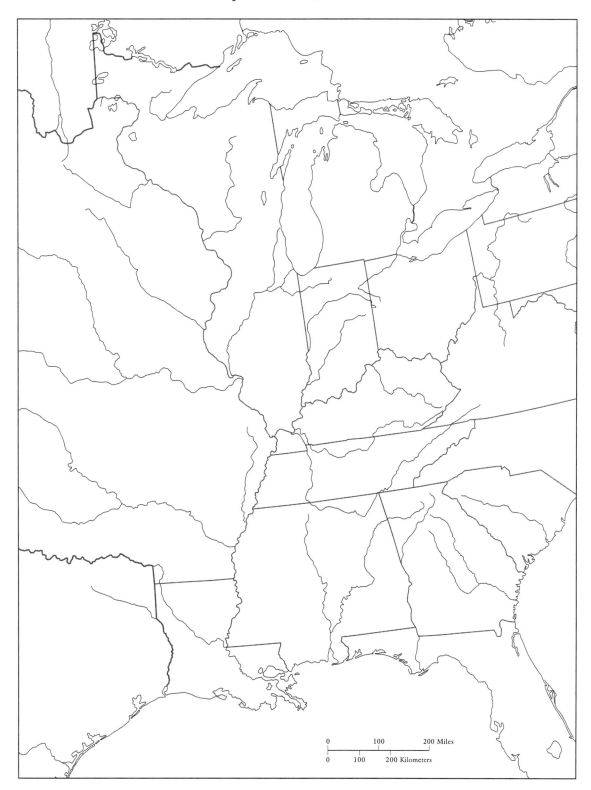

2. The "Five Civilized Tribes" controlled most of the southeastern United States. These tribes were the _____, _____, _____, _____, and the _____.

3. On the rice and cotton plantations of South Carolina and _____, slaves were worked utilizing the method known as the _____. This method of labor won for the slave the right to cultivate _____ of up to _____ acres.

4. By 1815 _____ had become America's largest city.

5. The United States had high levels of literacy; in 1790 about 85 percent of adult men in _____ and 60 percent in _____ and the _____ could read and write.

6. In 1790 only _____ granted the vote to all free men with no requirement for property ownership. After 1790 the new democracy, however, insisted upon equal rights for all white men, and so by 1840, only _____ kept a property qualification.

7. Between 1775 and 1820, states withdrew government support from religion. In the southern states the _____ Church declined in power; in New England _____ churches declined. The new denominations enjoying growth were the _____, _____, and _____.

Essay Question

1. Slavery represents the ultimate loss of liberty and equality and the almost total absence of power for those enslaved. After 1790, slave labor became less and less necessary in the Chesapeake. Refer to the maps entitled "Distribution of Slave Population, 1790–1820" on page 257 of *Liberty, Equality, Power* and discuss the reasons for that decline and the planters' response to this phenomenon.

Chapter 8
Completing the Revolution, 1789–1815

Chapter Summary

On April 30, 1789, George Washington's inauguration was held in New York City, the temporary capital of the United States. He, his advisors, and the elected congressmen faced the monumental task of establishing a balance between power and liberty after the Revolution.

The new Congress passed legislation that created the executive departments, levied imposts and excise taxes, adopted a Bill of Rights, and established a National Bank. Secretary of the Treasury Alexander Hamilton also devised a plan to absorb state Revolutionary War debts in exchange for establishing the nation's permanent capital along the Potomac River, a site chosen to placate the southern states.

In 1793, France and England resumed warfare against each other. Because of the Franco-American Alliance Treaty of 1778, the United States was pulled into the war, despite its proclamation of neutrality. Neither France nor England recognized the United States's neutrality.

Washington's new government saw four major issues arise in 1794. First, frontiersmen refused to pay the whiskey excise tax levied by Hamilton. Second, the Indians of the Northwest, with the help of the British, attacked American settlements. Third, as 90 percent of the nation's income came from trade with England, it was imperative to maintain friendly relations with that country. Finally, the border dispute between the United States and Spanish Florida needed to be resolved.

Washington sent federalized militia from Pennsylvania, Virginia, New Jersey, and Maryland into the western frontier to put down the Whiskey Rebellion. He also dispatched troops to put an end to the Indian-British threat in the Northwest. He then sent John Jay to negotiate a trade treaty with England. Jay's Treaty called for the removal of British troops from the Northwest forts in exchange for allowing small American ships to trade in the West Indies. The treaty was favored in the Northeast and by seaport cities; however, the South regarded it with contempt. At the same time, Thomas Pinckney was negotiating a treaty with Spain. Pinckney's Treaty drew the United States-Spanish Florida border in favor of the United States. Additionally, Spain relinquished claims to territory in the Southwest and gave Americans navigation rights on the Mississippi River and the right to deposit produce at New Orleans.

In the 1796 election, sectional political intrigue allowed the Federalist, John Adams, to become president with a Democratic-Republican, Thomas Jefferson, as his vice president. By the time Adams assumed the presidency, France had already broken off diplomatic relations with the United States. The young nation entered into a quasi-war with France in the Caribbean. Adams resolved the French crisis in 1800 without war but at great political cost to himself.

In the 1800 election, the Federalist Party's stronghold was the Northeast, but Adams had alienated many of his own party members. The Democratic–Republican party was quite strong in the South and its candidate, Thomas Jefferson, became president.

Jefferson authorized the $15 million purchase of the Louisiana Territory from Napoleon in 1803. The purchase doubled the size of the nation, assured the United States access to interior rivers such as the Missouri and Mississippi, and eliminated the French threat to the West.

The Napoleonic Wars began in 1803, again precluding American neutrality. "War Hawks" from the South and West pushed for a declaration of war against England in 1812. The war was supported in the South and West but not in the Northeast.

The United States attacked British Canada in 1812. Allied Indian and British forces, however, soon secured control of the Northwest. Tecumseh's confederacy also allied itself with the British in the hopes of driving out American settlers. In 1813, the Americans resumed the offensive against Canada, burning the Canadian capital of York. The next summer, the British retaliated, burning Washington, D.C., and unsuccessfully attacking Baltimore. In January 1815, Andrew Jackson led American forces in a victory at the Battle of New Orleans; however, the Treaty of Ghent had just been signed, ending the war before the battle. The treaty changed no borders and resolved no issues. It did, at least, end the war.

Map References

The exercises and questions in this chapter relate to the following maps and corresponding text in Chapter 8 of *Liberty, Equality, Power: A History of the American People.*

> Securing the West, 1790–1796 (p. 285)
>
> Presidential Election, 1800 (p. 291)
>
> Louisiana Purchase (p. 297)
>
> War of 1812 (p. 304)

Map Exercises

1. Label the following physical features on Map 8-A:
    a. Arkansas River
    b. Missouri River
    c. Mississippi River
    d. Rocky Mountains

Map 8-A: United States, circa 1804

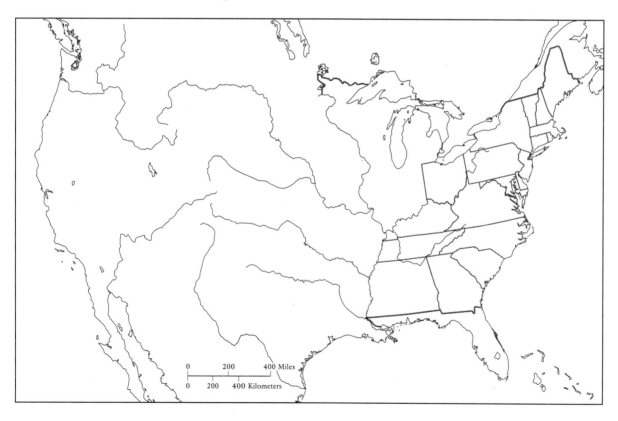

2. Label the following forts on Map 8-B:
    a. Fort Detroit
    b. Fort Dearborn
    c. Fort McHenry

3. Label the following bodies of water on Map 8-B:
    a. Lake Erie
    b. Lake Ontario
    c. Lake Champlain
    d. Chesapeake Bay
    e. Put-in-Bay

4. Indicate the locations and dates of the following battles on Map 8-B:
    a. Thames
    b. Horseshoe Bend
    c. Tippecanoe
    d. York
    e. New Orleans

Relating Maps and Text

1. When George Washington took the oath of office as the first president of the United States in 1789, the national capital was at _____. Under an agreement reached between Alexander Hamilton and congressional opposition, the capital was later moved to a site on the _____ River.

2. All of the southern states except _____ had paid off most of their Revolutionary War debts during the 1780s. Under Hamilton's plan, the federal government would assume state debts, causing money to flow into the _____.

3. In 1793 France, which was already at war with _____ and _____, declared war on _____.

4. _____ Treaty gave Americans the right to navigate the _____ and trans-ship produce at the Spanish port of _____.

5. The election of 1796 hinged on the electoral vote in _____ and _____. In the election of 1800, the one southern state in which John Adams had significant support was _____.

6. In 1803 President Thomas Jefferson sent delegates to Paris to negotiate the purchase of _____. Napoleon surprised the Americans by offering to sell the entire _____ for $15 million.

Map 8-B: War of 1812

7. Nearly all of the War Hawks, who called for war against Britain in the winter and spring of 1811–1812, were from the _____ or the _____. Among these congressmen were Henry Clay of _____, John C. Calhoun of _____, and George M. Troup of _____.

8. In 1812 American forces initiated an unsuccessful land invasion of _____. In the spring of 1813, United States forces burned the capital at _____, but an autumn offensive directed at _____ was unsuccessful.

9. The Indian leader _____ was killed at the battle of the _____ in October 1813.

10. As a result of their naval superiority along the Atlantic coast, the British were able to burn _____ and attack the larger city of _____ on the upper Chesapeake Bay.

11. The War of 1812 was ended by the Treaty of _____.

Essay Questions

1. From a geographical standpoint, why would the Louisiana Purchase cause northeasterners some concern?

2. Refer to the map entitled "War of 1812" on page 304 of *Liberty, Equality, Power* and explain the major geographical reason for the reluctance of the Northeast to declare war on Great Britain in June 1812.

Chapter 9
The Market Revolution, 1815–1860

Chapter Summary

Between 1815 and 1860, a revolution in the way Americans marketed agricultural products and manufactured goods swept the country. An emphasis on production for foreign markets became the new commercial creed of American manufacturing and farming interests.

Under the concept of Henry Clay's "American System," Congress chartered the Philadelphia-based Second Bank of the United States in 1816. This financial institution became the repository of government funds and regulated the issuance of bank notes by state banks. The following year, the Tariff of 1816 was implemented to protect American industry from foreign competition. Although the British blockade during the War of 1812 had demonstrated that the United States needed a dependable system of internal transportation, the government was reluctant to use federal funds to build roads within the individual states. As a result, before 1830 each state government funded the construction of canals, toll roads, and railroads within its borders.

Decisions of the Supreme Court of the United States during John Marshall's tenure improved the business environment. In the *Dartmouth College*, *McCulloch*, and *Gibbons* cases, the Marshall Court upheld the sanctity of corporate charters and contracts, upheld the right of the federal government to establish a National Bank and to be free of states' attempts to tax it, and affirmed federal jurisdiction over interstate commerce.

Transportation in America in 1815 was primitive, but steamboats, canals, and, eventually, railroads would trim travel time and shipping costs dramatically. Until 1840, the market revolution was a regional phenomenon, but after that date products went directly by canal and rail from the Northwest to the Northeast. The South was not included in direct trade.

The demand for meat products in northeastern urban centers prompted the New England states to shift to a cattle-raising farm economy, which contributed to massive deforestation. New Englanders concentrated on providing farm commodities for markets outside their traditional neighborhoods. In the Northwest by the 1830s, commercial wheat farms utilized mechanical agricultural innovations and exported their crops.

The industrial revolution that swept America's textile industry after 1800 began with the establishment of mill towns in Rhode Island in the late 18th century. Textile factories near Boston hired single women from farm communities to work in the highly mechanized mills, which catered to a predominantly domestic, not an international market. Merchants in seaport cities such as Boston and New York prospered in the import and export trade, but armies of low-paid women worked long hours in the garment and shoe-making trades.

Slave labor in the cotton plantations of the Old Southwest allowed the states of Alabama, Mississippi and Louisiana to grow more than half of the cotton produced in the United States by 1834. However, three-fourths of southern white families did not own slaves. Yeoman farmers produced primarily for home consumption and did not participate to any great extent in the market revolution occurring in the North.

From the 1830s on, a widening economic gap between the rich and the poor was much in evidence in America. That dichotomy existed in the North in the relationship between powerful factory owners and low-paid factory workers. It existed in the rural, agriculturally oriented South, not only in the relationship of master to slave, but also in the relationship between the powerful plantation owners who, by necessity, opted into the market revolution, and the yeoman farmer who, by choice, refused to participate.

Map Reference

The exercises and questions in this chapter relate to the following map and corresponding text in Chapter 9 of *Liberty, Equality, Power: A History of the American People.*

Rivers, Roads, and Canals, 1825–1860 (p. 317)

Map Exercises

1. Locate with a dot and label the following cities on Map 9:
   a. Philadelphia
   b. Baltimore
   c. New York City
   d. Buffalo
   e. Wheeling (VA)
   f. Rochester (NY)
   g. Pittsburgh
   h. Louisville
   i. St. Louis
   j. Worcester (MA)
   k. Providence (RI)
   l. Cincinnati
   m. Boston
   n. Lowell (MA)
   o. Chicago
   p. St. Augustine
   q. Charleston
   r. Richmond
   s. Cleveland
   t. New Orleans

2. Indicate with a bold line the routes of the following on Map 9:
   a. the National Road
   b. Erie Canal
   c. Coastal Road

3. Label the following rivers on Map 9:
   a. Illinois
   b. Wabash
   c. Ohio

Map 9: United States during the Market Revolution

Relating Maps and Text

1. The Second Bank of the United States was headquartered in the city of _____. The Supreme Court case of _____ upheld the constitutionality of the Bank and denied a state's right to tax a federal agency.

2. Until about 1830, most westerners settled near tributaries of the _____ system. The _____ made commercial agriculture feasible in the West.

3. The _____ covered 364 miles between the cities of _____ and _____. It drove down the cost of transportation and led to the growth of market towns and new cities like _____, _____, and _____.

4. In the 1840s and 1850s the transportation networks linking the urban centers of the _____ and _____ with the commercial farms of the _____ made both areas less dependent upon the _____.

5. By the 1820s and 1830s New England's cash "crop" had become _____; however, this transition resulted in _____.

6. During the 1820s New York City became the center of a national market selling _____. This new market was made possible because of the availability of cheap _____ and cheap _____.

7. The South's emphasis on an agricultural economy can be illustrated by comparing the agricultural work force of the South to that of the North. In 1800, _____ percent of the southern and _____ percent of the northern work force were employed in agriculture; by 1860 that proportion had changed to _____ percent of the northern and _____ percent of the southern work force.

Essay Questions

1. Why was there more canal construction in the Ohio River valley and Old Northwest in the 1830s and 1840s than in the southern states?

2. Why did the Industrial Revolution that transformed the northeastern cities fail to have the same effect in the South?

Chapter 10
Toward an American Culture

Chapter Summary

After 1815, Americans began to move out of the cultural shadow of Europe and to create their own distinct social patterns, literary and artistic styles, forms of recreation and entertainment, and even religions. Although there were many exceptions, the emerging American culture was generally republican, capitalist, and Protestant.

Members of the northern middle class, the beneficiaries of the market revolution, embraced manufacturing and commercial farming. They also linked marketplace ideas of personal success and individual autonomy with the tenets of the new evangelical religions that swept the country after 1830. In business, as in religious life, they thought, one could reap the rewards of making good moral choices. Charles Grandison Finney and other revivalist preachers provided the theological bases for this linkage by stressing the importance of human free choice in bringing about the Millennium.

Economic and religious ideas also contributed to a change in middle-class family relationships. Men worked outside the home; women stayed behind, taking care of the children and the household. Domestic life thus became more feminized. Popular, sentimental literature reflected this altered role, glorifying women as moral leaders in family and society—and often portraying them as victims of male domination. The most successful of these sentimental novels was Harriet Beecher Stowe's *Uncle Tom's Cabin* (1852).

Evangelical Christianity and sentimental literature drew on emotions; so, too, did a new American tradition in the fine arts that emerged between 1830 and 1860. Nature and the wilderness became moral teachers, things of sublime beauty, not dark forces to be feared. Mount Auburn Cemetery, established near Boston in 1831, reflected this new view of nature: its paths followed the contours of the land, and natural vegetation was retained. Niagara Falls, combining beauty and incredible power, became the first major tourist destination in the United States after the Erie Canal made it more accessible to travelers in 1825.

The "plain people" of the North—the farmers and laborers who had either not benefited from the market revolution or had in fact been hurt economically by it—rejected the middle class's optimistic ideas of free agency and personal choice. Many retained their belief in an uncontrollable, unknowable providence. Some became convinced that Christ's Second Coming was imminent, especially when religious leaders such as William Miller "proved" as much through detailed biblical analysis. Joseph Smith, the founder of the Church of Jesus Christ of Latter-Day Saints, responded to the market revolution and its feminization of domestic and social life by establishing a faith centered on a male-dominated hierarchy and the idealization of farming.

Northern popular culture was based in the cities. Young men might crowd a tavern to watch and wager on cockfights, boxing matches, death matches between large animals, or other violent events. Theater became democratized, and different tastes sometimes led to violent confrontations between poorer members of the audience and their more wealthy counterparts in the boxes. New forms of popular entertainment emerged, most notably the minstrel show, in which white entertainers donned black makeup and portrayed stereotypical African Americans in a formulaic show. New technology drove down prices of newspapers and books, which began to reach a broader audience in the 1830s and 1840s. Stories were often sensationalized tales of violence and sex, good versus evil.

In the South, society remained much more conservative and localistic. To white southerners, the North's individual autonomy meant selfishness: the ideal man or woman maintained the family honor and played a prescribed social role.

Leisure activities reflected the localism of the South. Drinking, dancing, wrestling, corn-husking, hunting, fishing, and Bible reading filled much of southerners' leisure time. Commercial entertainment such as theater, horse racing, and minstrel shows could be found only in the cities and along the major rivers. New Orleans became the horse racing capital of the United States, and it was the only city in the South where professional prizefights were held.

Evangelical Protestantism swept the South in the early decades of the 19th century, and by 1860 almost 90 percent of church members there were Methodist, Presbyterian, Baptist, or Disciples of Christ. Southern evangelicalism was based not on individual autonomy but rather on acceptance of God's will. Disease, death in the family, a poor crop: all were signs of God's will, and all served to remind southern Christians of their own lack of power. As the South became the distinct slaveholding region of the United States, religion was enlisted in its defense. The Bible, with its references to slavery, became a source of proslavery arguments. Slaveholders also portrayed slavery as a good thing for the slaves: it exposed them to Christianity and thus offered them a chance for eternal life.

For their part, slaves adapted Christianity to their own experience and needs. They were the chosen people of God; America was Egypt, out of which God would deliver them; Moses was, after Jesus, the central figure of the Bible. For some Christian slaves, Christianity promised success for revolt and a violent end to slavery. Denmark Vesey, who planned a revolt in 1822, equated Charleston with Jericho and South Carolina with Egypt; nine years later, Nat Turner used his religious visions to recruit fellow rebels and to justify the slaughter of whites.

As American culture developed in the early decades of the 19th century, it did so in a society in which liberty and power continued to be distributed unequally. Social and regional differences were growing more marked, and violence was often regarded as a logical response to those differences.

Relating Geography and Text

1. _____ was the first center of factory production in the United States.

2. Charles Grandison Finney led a six-month religious revival in the city of _____ beginning in November 1830.

3. The Mount Auburn Cemetery near Boston revealed a new perception of nature. The cities of _____ and _____, among others, copied the idea for their cemeteries.

4. In the 1820s Americans began to travel to view scenery. Favorite scenic locations included the _____ River valley, the _____, the _____ Mountains, and, especially, _____, on the border between the United States and Canada.

5. Denmark Vesey, a free black man from _____, planned a slave rebellion in 1822, but the plan was betrayed by slaves before it could start. The revolt led by Nat Turner in 1831 in _____, however, did occur, and resulted in the deaths of 55 whites and the execution of Turner and his followers.

Essay Questions

1. Discuss ways in which transportation shaped cultural life in the United States between 1815 and 1860.

2. If you have access to the Internet, search for information on Mount Auburn Cemetery. What did the builders of this cemetery hope to achieve (besides providing a place to bury the dead)? What evidence can you find that indicates that they succeeded?

Chapter 11
Society, Culture, and Politics, 1820s–1840s

Chapter Summary

By the 1830s, the two-party system was entrenched in American politics. The Whigs and the Democrats each found support throughout the nation. Their constituencies held particular ideologies more than they reflected different geographic regions; however, there were signs of growing geographic sectionalism in antebellum America.

The two parties offered opposing ideas concerning government interaction with the people. Northern as well as southern beneficiaries of the market revolution favored the Whig Party philosophy, which demanded government involvement in the nation's economic development. In contrast, northern and southern Democrats wanted greater personal freedom and less government interference.

Banking and the financing of internal improvements were two economic issues on which party lines were decisively drawn. The Whigs favored an elastic currency and saw a relationship between moral progress and the market society. Therefore, they supported government-regulated banks and federally financed internal improvements. Democrats tended to favor "hard money," and they disapproved of federal money being appropriated to finance local or state roads and canals.

By the 1830s, political preferences were also expressed about social issues such as education, prisons, asylum reform, alcoholic consumption, and slavery. Northern Whigs favored government involvement in improving the morality of the people. Northern Democrats disagreed, arguing that a government cannot and should not legislate morality. In the South, however, Whigs and Democrats stood together on social issues such as education and temperance. Consequently, sectional lines between the North and South were becoming stronger than party lines in the South. The North was leading the way to reform while the South was leading the resistance to change.

Antebellum America was split sectionally over racial issues as well. By 1804, nearly every Northern state had either outlawed slavery or had made provisions for gradual emancipation. Therefore, by 1830 there were relatively few slaves remaining in the North, and there was a sizable and growing free black population. Along with this came a growing pattern of discrimination against African Americans in the northern states.

By the 1830s, the abolitionist movement was becoming more popular in the North. The American Colonization Society attempted to relocate blacks to Liberia, Africa, with little success. During the antebellum period individuals such as William Lloyd Garrison and organizations such as the American Anti-Slavery Society made the question of slavery an issue of national debate. The North viewed slavery as a part of the civil liberties issue, but to the South it was more a question of political power.

Middle-class women in the North often progressed from advocating moral reforms, particularly the abolition of slavery, to championing women's rights. The first women's rights convention was held in 1848, with delegates emphasizing political rights, especially the right to vote. Suffrage symbolized liberty and equality, and it conferred political power on its possessor.

Map Reference

The exercises and questions in this chapter relate to the text of Chapter 11 of *Liberty, Equality, Power: A History of the American People* and the following map.

Free and Slave States and Territories, 1848 (p. 437)

Map Exercises

1. Label the following states on Map 11:
    a.   Michigan
    b.   Vermont
    c.   Wisconsin
    d.   New York
    e.   Ohio
    f.   Maine
    g.   Maryland
    h.   Delaware
    i.   Georgia
    j.   Kentucky
    k.   Arkansas

Map 11: United States, circa 1840

Relating Maps and Text

1. In the 1830s wealthy urban merchants were most likely to be supporters of the _____ Party. Urban Irish immigrants, on the other hand, would most likely have been backers of the _____ Party.

2. In the 1830s, the control of banks was a major social and political issue. The states of _____, _____, _____, _____, and _____ chose to provide state-owned banks. The state of _____ passed the Safety-Fund Law in 1829 to provide insurance for depositors if a bank failed.

3. The most advanced, expensive, and centralized state school systems were established in the states of _____, _____, and _____ under the leadership of Whig reformers.

4. Prisons built in the cities of _____ and _____ in the 1820s reflected the idea that prisoners should be placed in solitary cells to contemplate their errors and to plan for a better future. In the state of _____, prisoners came together for meals and work but were forbidden to speak to one another.

5. In an effort to eliminate public drinking establishments, _____ passed a law allowing merchants to sell liquor only in quantities of more than 15 gallons. By the 1850s states began to pass prohibition laws; _____ passed the first such state law in 1851.

6. The first major American race riot occurred in the city of _____ in 1834.

7. The _____ proposed the return of free blacks to West Africa and transported a few thousand to _____. A more severe blow to American slavery came in 1830 when _____ freed the slaves in its Caribbean possessions. The next year, William Lloyd Garrison published the first issue of _____. The greatest support for abolition came from _____, _____, _____, and the middle classes in the northeastern cities.

8. John H. Noyes established a community in _____, New York, that practiced plural marriage.

9. The first Women's Rights Convention, held at _____, New York, in 1848, called for _____ rights for women.

Essay Question

1. Why was there a greater emphasis on public school education in the North than in the South?

Harcourt Brace & Company

Chapter 12
Jacksonian Democracy

Chapter Summary

American expansion west of the Mississippi began after the Louisiana Purchase. Explorers led the way. Departing from St. Louis in May 1804, Lewis and Clark led 41 members of the Corps of Discovery up the Missouri River, across the Rocky Mountains, and down the Snake and Columbia Rivers to the Pacific Ocean, which they reached in November 1805. Whites were also filtering into the southern portions of the Louisiana Purchase: New Orleans and the Arkansas and Missouri Territories. At the same time, the Sioux Nation was on the move into southern Nebraska and west to the Yellowstone River.

In 1819, Missouri's petition for admission into the Union was initially stymied by the ill-fated Tallmadge Amendments, legislation designed to bestow statehood upon Missouri only if it became a free state. By 1820, Congress had resolved the stalemate by passing the Missouri Compromise. Maine entered the Union as a free state, and Missouri entered as a slave state.

The financial Panic of 1819 (caused partly by fraudulent banking practices and partly by a reduced demand in Europe for American food products) resulted in massive unemployment, failed businesses, and a general economic depression. Out of the financial chaos, however, Martin Van Buren forged a new coalition of northern and southern agrarians into the Democratic Party, which dominated American politics through the 1820s and 1830s.

The election of 1824 pitted the Northeast's John Quincy Adams against a field of Southerners and Westerners, including Andrew Jackson of Tennessee. The outcome of the race hinged upon the support of Henry Clay, whose political strength in the Northwest threw the election to Adams. Jackson decried the "Corrupt Bargain" and planned his revenge for the next presidential election.

The election of 1828 saw the emergence of the Jacksonian Democratic Party with its power base centered in the South and West. Adams's victory in New England was not enough to keep Jackson from the presidency.

The first major issue to arise during the Jackson administration was the Tariff of 1828. Southerners considered the import tax, which they called the "Tariff of Abominations," an unfair burden on them and a benefit to the Northeast and Old Northwest. South Carolina, led by Vice President John C. Calhoun, argued that states had the right to nullify federal laws within their own borders. Jackson, no supporter of the tariff but firmly dedicated to the Union, nearly used military force to control the South Carolinians, but a compromise was reached before coercion was necessary.

Also during the Jackson presidency, the liberty of southern Indian tribes was compromised by several southern states, including Georgia. Jackson would not protect the sovereignty of the tribes within the states, and his refusal led to the Indian Removal Act of 1830. Martin Van Buren, Jackson's successor, oversaw the removal of the Cherokee from Georgia to Oklahoma in 1838 across the "Trail of Tears."

By the election of 1836, the Whig Party had coalesced into a political faction critical of what it regarded as Jackson's tyrannical use of the presidential veto power, his "hard money" philosophy, and his war on the Bank of the United States. Democratic candidate Van Buren nevertheless won the election. After a spirited campaign, the election of 1840 elevated the Whig William Henry Harrison to the presidency, as the political power struggle between Whigs and Jacksonian Democrats reached its highest point.

Map References

The exercises and questions in this chapter relate to the text of Chapter 12 of *Liberty, Equality, Power: A History of the American People* and the following maps.

  Presidential Election, 1824 (p. 408)
  Presidential Election, 1828 (p. 413)
  Overland Trails, 1846 (p. 439)

Map Exercises

1. Label the following rivers on Map 12:
  a. Missouri
  b. Snake
  c. Columbia

2. Label the following states on Map 12:
  a. Alabama
  b. Illinois
  c. Maine
  d. Missouri
  e. Indiana
  f. Mississippi

3. Shade in and label the following territories (as of 1828) on Map 12:
  a. Arkansas Territory
  b. Florida Territory
  c. Oregon Country

4. Draw in the 36°30′ N latitude line on Map 12.

Relating Maps and Text

1. Under the Missouri Compromise of 1820, the northern counties of _____ became the free state of _____, and _____ was admitted to the Union as a slave state. Slavery was excluded north of latitude _____ North.

2. The Panic of 1819 had two major international causes: (1) a shortage of precious metals from _____ and _____ and (2) hoarding of available specie in _____. In the United States, bankers and businessmen expanded _____ and issued _____.

3. In 1824, presidential candidate Andrew Jackson was best known for his activities in the South and West: he came from the state of _____, had fought Indians in the South and the British at _____ in the War of 1812, and had led an invasion of _____ in 1818.

Map 12: United States, circa 1848

4. In the elections of 1824 and 1828, John Quincy Adams carried _____, and Andrew Jackson's strength was in the _____ and _____.

5. In the British-American Conventions of 1818, the United States-Canadian boundary was extended west to the _____. The next year, the Adams-Onis Treaty gave the United States title to _____ and established American claims to the _____.

6. The Monroe Doctrine recognized the independence of the _____ and outlawed colonization of the Americas by _____ powers. The real enforcement power of the Monroe Doctrine lay in the _____ navy.

7. In the 1820s the state of _____ began seizing Indian lands and turning them over to white farmers.

8. The state of _____ nullified the federal tariffs of 1828 and 1832 and precipitated a power struggle with President Andrew Jackson.

9. During the Panic of 1837 _____ cities were particularly affected by high unemployment and business closures.

Essay Question

1. Give three examples of Andrew Jackson's use of presidential powers that impinged upon the liberty of his adversaries.

Chapter 13

Manifest Destiny: An Empire for Liberty—or Slavery?

Chapter Summary

From its beginnings in the early seventeenth century as a British possession, the United States was marked by expansion and growth. The acquisition of Florida from Spain, close on the heels of the Louisiana Purchase, capped the annexation record of the United States's first fifty years, and seemingly provided the young nation with enough land for settlers to last another fifty years. So strong was the fever to increase the territorial size of the United States that a contemporary journalist attributed the nation's inexorable movement to the Pacific as its "Manifest Destiny." The future of slavery in the trans-Mississippi region appeared to be settled by the Missouri Compromise of 1820.

By the early 1840s, however, both territorial expansion and the question of the right of slave owners to take their slaves west of the Mississippi, by way of the Oregon Trail or other overland routes, moved to the center of political debate. The intense controversies generated by the latter continued until the Civil War erupted at Fort Sumter.

The American Indians' nonstop retreat from the Atlantic Coast would finally come to an end on the Great Plains. There was nowhere else to go. In the Southwestern section of the present United States, the Indians coexisted with the Hispanic descendants of the first Europeans to colonize the New World.

The Indians and Hispanics were not the only losers in the Anglo-American's insatiable appetite for western lands. The wives, daughters, and other female relatives of American pioneers rarely had a say in the decision to move west, but they always got their share of the hardships of living in the wilderness. The Mormons, who settled the Salt Lake basin in 1847 hoping that their flight from persecution would end there, established a particularly patriarchal society in the West.

Two regions, Oregon and Texas, brought the United States into serious conflict with other nations. A compromise ended the talk of war with England over possession of the Oregon country. The annexation of Texas in 1845, combined with a dispute over the Rio Grande boundary between Mexico and Texas, and President Polk's ambition to acquire California and the vast New Mexico territory, led to a war between the United States and Mexico. The war gained for the United States the disputed region of southern Texas, New Mexico, and California. It also helped to rekindle the not-quite-dormant slavery controversy. Antislavery congressmen pushed for passage of the Wilmot Proviso, which would have prohibited slavery in any territory gained from Mexico.

After the discovery of gold near Sacramento in 1848 touched off a massive migration of miners, settlers, entrepreneurs, and others to the gold fields, already populous California sought admission to the Union as a free state. Since statehood for California would give the free states a one-state advantage in the Senate, the South demurred. Losing numerical equality in the Senate would only amplify other southern concerns, such as federal threats to slavery and the slow stream of slaves escaping to the North and Canada. As southerners openly discussed secession in 1850, the separate sections of the Compromise of 1850 cleared both houses of Congress and were signed by the president.

The Compromise eased tensions in the short run, but some of its provisions actually heightened the sectional conflict. The Fugitive Slave Act did not reduce the number of slaves escaping every year, for more and more people in the North gave assistance to the escapees. Moreover, public reaction against slavery intensified at each of the few times officials recaptured escaped slaves in the North. Meanwhile, in the 1850s, southern expansionists cast their eyes on Cuba and Nicaragua. Cuba, in particular, attracted the attention of slaveholders, and the willingness of American diplomats to use force, as evidenced by the Ostend Manifesto, caused an international scandal. By the mid-1850s, the expansionist voice of the nation had a distinctly southern accent.

Map References

The exercises and questions in this chapter relate to the following maps and corresponding text in Chapter 13 of *Liberty, Equality, Power: A History of the American People*.

> Free and Slave States and Territories, 1848 (p. 437)
>
> Overland Trails, 1846 (p. 439)
>
> Settlement of the Oregon Boundary Dispute, 1846 (p. 444)
>
> Principal Campaigns of the Mexican War, 1846–1847 (p. 447)

Map Exercises

1. Label the following on Map 13:
   a. Missouri
   b. Arkansas
   c. Iowa
   d. Texas
   e. 49th Parallel
   f. Mexican Cession

2. Locate with a dot and label the following cities and forts on Map 13:
   a. Santa Fe
   b. Independence
   c. San Antonio
   d. Ft. Leavenworth
   e. Vera Cruz
   f. Monterey (CA)
   g. Mexico City
   h. San Francisco
   i. Sutter's Fort
   j. Nauvoo
   k. Salt Lake City
   l. Portland (OR)

3. Locate and label with dates the following battles on Map 13:
   a. Monterrey (Mexico)
   b. Buena Vista
   c. Cerro Gordo
   d. Chapultepec

4. Locate or draw in and label the following rivers on Map 13:
   a. Nueces
   b. Rio Grande
   c. Columbia
   d. Willamette

Map 13: Western United States in the 1840s

e.   Colorado
f.   Missouri

Relating Maps and Text

1. In the 1840s, the United States government decided to create a "permanent Indian frontier" at about the _____.

2. Between 1803 and 1846, territorial additions brought the states of _____, _____, _____, _____ ,_____ and _____ into the Union as well as parts of _____ and _____. Of these, only _____ was a free state.

3. The six-month trek over the Oregon Trail during the 1840s brought many settlers to the _____ River valley south of the Columbia River.

4. In the 1830s, American merchants traveled the _____ Trail, bringing American manufactured goods to New Mexico. The California Trail ended at _____.

5. _____ served as the governor of the Utah Territory from 1850 to 1857.

6. By 1835 there were _____ Americans in Texas, mostly in the _____ part of that Mexican territory. The next year, delegates from across Texas declared its independence. At a battle on the _____, the revolutionary forces captured _____ and forced him to sign a treaty granting Texas its independence.

7. In the 1844 presidential election, James K. Polk ran on a platform calling for the annexation of _____ and the acquisition of _____ to the Alaskan border.

8. In August 1846, during the Mexican War, General Stephen Kearny's army occupied _____. Colonel Alexander Doniphan occupied _____, and in the spring of 1847 linked up with Zachary Taylor's army at _____, Mexico. Taylor's forces won a hard-fought battle at _____ on February 22 and 23, 1847.

9. General Winfield Scott led an Army-Navy force against the Mexican coastal fortress at _____ in March 1847. He marched west and captured _____ in September.

10. The free state of _____ joined the Union as part of the Compromise of 1850.

11. Two countries that attracted the attention of filibustering expeditions in the 1840s and 1850s were _____ and _____.

Essay Questions

1. Of what strategic importance was the settlement of the Oregon boundary dispute in 1846? How did the settlement threaten the liberty of the original inhabitants of the area?

2. In what ways was the Compromise of 1850 a true compromise? What aspect of the Compromise threatened the liberty of a segment of the American population?

Harcourt Brace & Company

Chapter 14
The Gathering Tempest, 1853–1860

Chapter Summary

The 1850s were an era of growth in population and in prejudice. Between 1845 and 1855 about 3 million immigrants came to the United States, mostly from Ireland and Germany. Many of these immigrants became naturalized and active in the Democratic Party. A majority of the Irish Catholics settled in northeastern cities, and American nativism became most active in that area.

The 1850s also saw the growth of sectional strife and its expansion into the western plains. The Nebraska Territory was organized in 1853, but proslavery forces demanded the repeal of the Missouri Compromise of 1820 and the creation of two territories. The one west of Missouri was to be known as Kansas, and the one west of Iowa and Minnesota as Nebraska. According to the Kansas-Nebraska Act of 1854, the issue of slavery in those territories would be resolved by popular sovereignty.

In 1856, civil war erupted in Kansas. Proslavery Missourians sacked Lawrence and murdered several free-state settlers. In retaliation, John Brown and his supporters attacked a proslavery settlement at Pottawatomie Creek, killing five men. This incident was followed by an onslaught of raids and murders that subsided only when federal troops were sent to Kansas.

In the 1856 election, the newly formed Republican Party, composed of old Free-Soilers, former Whigs, and antislavery Democrats, ran John C. Frémont for the presidency. The Democratic candidate, James Buchanan, won by carrying the southern states as well as Pennsylvania, New Jersey, Illinois, Indiana, and California.

The Supreme Court blocked efforts to obtain liberty for slaves brought into free states and territories when it decided the Dred Scott case in 1857. The Taney Court determined that sections of the Missouri Compromise were unconstitutional, as they denied citizens the right to their property without due process by prohibiting slavery in territories north of 36°30'. Furthermore, the Court declared that blacks were not citizens and, therefore, not entitled to bring suit in a court of law.

Meanwhile, in Kansas, minority proslavery forces had pushed through the Lecompton Constitution, which legalized slavery in that territory. After much debate, Kansas voters rejected the constitution. However, the split in the Democratic Party between southerners and northerners over the slave issue was growing.

In 1859, John Brown attempted to destroy slavery in the South. He and his followers attacked the federal arsenal at Harpers Ferry, Virginia, intending to use the munitions to arm slaves against their white masters. However, troops led by Colonel Robert E. Lee and Lieutenant J.E.B. Stuart arrested Brown and his men, and Brown was executed.

The 1850s were also a time of great economic growth and prosperity. Railroad construction in the Old Northwest brought that region and the Northeast closer economically. At the same time, the division between the North and the South was intensifying. In the North, farming was still the leading industry, but an increase of manufacturing industries rapidly diversified that region's economy. In contrast, the South was primarily agricultural, with cotton, tobacco, and sugar as its major crops.

In defense of slavery, the South argued that black slaves had a higher standard of living than northern factory wage earners. However, wages were on the rise, and job opportunities were plentiful in the North as compared to the rest of the world. As the decade of the 1850s drew to a close, the South was determined to use its power to maintain slavery. The North, on the other hand, was just as determined to use its power to liberate the slave population.

Map References

The exercises and questions in this chapter are related to the following maps and corresponding text in Chapter 14 of *Liberty, Equality, Power: A History of the American People.*

> Kansas-Nebraska and the Slavery Issue (p. 475)
>
> Main Transportation Routes in the 1850s (p. 482)
>
> Slavery and Staple Crops in the South, 1860 (p. 487)

Map Exercises

1. Label the following on Map 14:
   a. Wisconsin
   b. Cincinnati
   c. Missouri
   d. Lawrence (KS)
   e. Pottawatomie Creek
   f. Indiana
   g. Chicago

2. Identify the following territories on Map 14:
   a. Nebraska
   b. Minnesota
   c. Kansas
   d. Utah
   e. New Mexico
   f. Oregon
   g. Washington
   h. Indian

Relating Maps and Text

1. Abraham Lincoln returned to politics as a result of the _____. He argued that the contention that slavery would not spread to _____ because of its climate was untrue.

2. The American Party, or _____, did well in the midterm elections of 1854, especially in the _____ and the _____.

3. Senator David Atchison of _____ worried that if slavery was kept out of _____, then it would be abolished in _____, _____, _____, and all the territories.

4. Dred Scott's owner had lived in _____ and the _____ before returning the slave to _____.

Harcourt Brace & Company

Map 14: United States, circa 1856

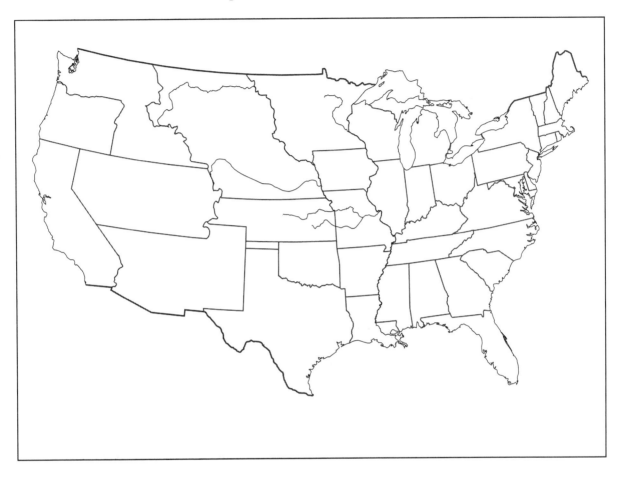

5. The expansion of railroad building in the _____ in the 1850s linked the region more closely to the _____ and allowed _____ to become the terminus of numerous railroad lines.

6. By the 1850s nearly three-fourths of the public school teachers in _____ were women.

7. Between 1845 and 1855, the price of cotton and slaves _____. Southern crops accounted for _____ of all U.S. exports.

8. By 1860, the North had _____ times more industrial output per capita than the South. _____ percent of northerners were farmers, but its _____ and _____ work force almost _____ that of agriculture.

9. Commercial conventions in the South in the 1850s called for the annexation of _____ with its productive agricultural economy and large slave population.

10. Seven-eighths of the 4 million immigrants who came to America between 1845 and 1860 settled in the free states to take advantage of better _____ and _____.

11. After his attack on the federal arsenal at _____, John Brown hoped to move southward along the _____ and free the slaves.

Essay Questions

1. Taking the geography of the area into consideration, why would slave-holding citizens of Missouri in 1853 want slavery to exist in the proposed Nebraska Territory?

2. Compare and contrast the various forms of power that the North and the South had in the late 1850s.

Chapter 15
Secession and Civil War, 1860–1862

Chapter Summary

The United States faced its greatest challenge in the tumultuous years of the 1860s. The presidential election of 1860 reflects the turbulent times. The Democratic Party's first attempt at nominating a presidential candidate in Charleston failed. A second attempt was made in Baltimore, where the party split into two factions: the Southern Rights Democratic Party, which nominated John C. Breckinridge of Kentucky, and the regular Democrats, who chose Stephen Douglas. A coalition of former Whigs backed Tennessean John Bell. And the Republicans, meeting in Chicago, nominated Abraham Lincoln. In the election, Breckinridge carried the eleven slave states, while Douglas and Bell diluted the power of the Democratic Party. Lincoln, consequently, won the electoral vote by carrying the North and became president.

By February 1861, the United States of America no longer stood united. In response to Lincoln's election, seven of the southern states seceded from the Union between December 1860 and February 1861, when they formed the Confederate States of America and established a capital at Montgomery, Alabama. In the meantime, the Congress, in an attempt to hold the Union together, debated the Crittenden Compromise. Because it required northern Republicans to make all of the concessions and to repudiate the platform on which they had won the presidency, however, it failed to receive congressional approval.

Jefferson Davis, the moderate secessionist president of the Confederacy, knew that the South needed the remaining eight slave states to join the cause if the Confederacy were to survive. But before any other states seceded from the Union, the first shots of the Civil War were fired in South Carolina. On April 12, 1861, as ships approached to resupply Fort Sumter in Charleston harbor, Confederate troops opened fire upon the fort, and the war began. Shortly thereafter, Virginia, Arkansas, Tennessee, and North Carolina joined the Confederacy. The border states of Maryland, Delaware, Kentucky, and Missouri remained loyal to the Union.

The first military campaign after Fort Sumter took place in 1861 in northern Virginia. The Confederacy shocked the North by soundly defeating the Union Army at Bull Run. However, the North rebounded quickly, taking New Orleans in April 1862 and following up with victories at Fort Henry on the Tennessee River and Fort Donelson on the Cumberland. Another important Union victory occurred in April at the Battle of Shiloh in Tennessee.

The Confederacy was not, however, losing every battle. In June 1862, Confederate forces drove the Union Army from Richmond after the Union had laid siege to the city. Additionally, in August 1862, the South won the Second Battle of Bull Run, and Lee invaded Maryland on September 4. Victory for either side at this point seemed uncertain.

The liberty of the Southern states to secede from the Union and form their own nation was challenged by the North's military in 1861 and 1862. The South used its own military power to attempt to confirm its existence and freedom, and by September 1862, Richmond was anticipating European aid in affirming its liberty.

Map References

The exercises and questions in this chapter relate to the following maps and corresponding text in Chapter 15 of *Liberty, Equality, Power: A History of the American People.*

Map Exercises

1. Label the following states on Map 15:
    a. Pennsylvania
    b. Illinois
    c. Indiana
    d. Virginia
    e. Kentucky
    f. Tennessee
    g. Missouri
    h. South Carolina
    i. Georgia
    j. Mississippi
    k. Florida
    l. Alabama
    m. Louisiana
    n. Delaware
    o. Maryland
    p. West Virginia

2. Locate and label the following rivers on Map 15:
    a. Mississippi
    b. Tennessee
    c. Cumberland
    d. Savannah
    e. York
    f. James
    g. Potomac
    h. Ohio

3. Locate with a dot and label the following cities on Map 15:
    a. Charleston
    b. Montgomery
    c. Springfield
    d. Norfolk
    e. Savannah
    f. New Orleans
    g. Cairo
    h. Memphis
    i. Vicksburg
    j. Baton Rouge

Harcourt Brace & Company

Map 15: Civil War, 1860–1862

- k. Corinth
- l. Nashville
- m. Washington, D.C.
- n. Richmond

4. Locate and label the following battles on Map 15:
- a. Bull Run
- b. Fort Donelson
- c. Shiloh
- d. Seven Days

Relating Maps and Text

1. As the 1860 presidential election approached, three states that were crucial to Lincoln's success were _____, _____, and _____.

2. The first three southern states to secede from the Union in 1860–1861 were _____, _____, and _____.

3. The five border states that supported the Union during the Civil War were _____, _____, _____, _____, and _____.

4. Guerrilla warfare and a civil war within the Civil War characterized the state of _____ from 1861–1864.

5. In Indian Territory, members of the "five civilized tribes" tended to side with the _____ during the Civil War.

6. Through "King Cotton diplomacy," the Confederacy hoped to secure an alliance with _____.

7. In northern Virginia, the Union Army's movements were hampered in the spring of 1862 by several rivers that flowed from _____ to _____ between Washington and _____.

8. In February 1862, Union Army and Navy successes at Fort _____ on the _____ River and Fort _____ on the Cumberland River resulted in the surrender of _____, the first Confederate state capital to fall to Union forces.

Essay Question

1. Confederate naval power was never equal to the Union's. However, for the first year of the war, the Union naval blockade was fairly ineffective. What are the geographic and military reasons for this, and why did the South fail to take greater advantage of the ineffectiveness?

Chapter 16
A New Birth of Freedom, 1862–1865

Chapter Summary

The fate of slavery in the South was paramount in the minds of many northern politicians by the end of 1861. Slaves provided the main labor force of the Confederacy. To attack the South's war effort by freeing or confiscating that labor force was a viable aspect of total war.

In 1862, with Lincoln's approval, Congress passed a resolution offering compensation to any border states that would abolish slavery. Even with Lincoln's urging, the border states did not accept the Union offer of compensated emancipation. Lincoln then decided to issue an emancipation proclamation as soon as the Union Army could give him significant military victories to support the proclamation.

That opportunity came after the one-day battle of Antietam, Maryland, on September 17, 1862, a bloody day that saw 23,000 casualties between the two sides. Although the battle was a draw, Robert E. Lee's army retreated into Virginia, making it appear to be a Union victory. Lincoln used it as the opportunity to issue his preliminary Emancipation Proclamation, announcing that slaves in areas still in rebellion as of January 1, 1863, would be "forever free." However, U. S. Grant's inability to take Vicksburg in November 1862, and Ambrose Burnside's failure to dislodge Lee from Fredericksburg, Virginia, on December 13, 1862, marked the beginning of a series of Union defeats that brought despondency to Lincoln and supporters of the Northern cause.

In May 1863, at the battle of Chancellorsville, Lee's army drove Union forces under General Joe Hooker back across the Rappahannock River. The next month, Lee moved north into Pennsylvania, but between July 1 and July 3 he was unable to dislodge the Union forces of General George G. Meade at Gettysburg.

In the West, Grant's army at Vicksburg finally obtained the surrender of that key Mississippi River garrison town on July 4 after a three-month siege. Several days later, Port Hudson, the last Confederate bastion on the river, fell to Union forces. On September 20 at Chickamauga, Confederate forces pushed the enemy back to Chattanooga, but two months later Joe Hooker's Union troops drove General Braxton Bragg's Confederates off Missionary Ridge and twenty miles south into Georgia.

By the spring of 1864, Grant was ready to move into Virginia against Lee. However, the Union commander's unsuccessful efforts to drive Lee's army from the field at the Wilderness, Spotsylvania, and Cold Harbor between May 5 and June 3 produced enormous casualties on both sides. Grant's attempt to take Petersburg, Virginia, the key to Richmond, from June 15 to June 18, produced no more positive results than did Spotsylvania or Cold Harbor. General Benjamin Butler's attack on Richmond up the James River was also a failure.

The tide of the war turned to favor the North in early July when William Tecumseh Sherman's Union forces drove Joseph E. Johnston back to less than five miles from Atlanta. Even though the Confederates were entrenched outside the city for three months, Atlanta was abandoned to the Union on September 2, 1864. That same month, General Philip Sheridan undertook a scorched-earth policy in the Shenandoah Valley, burning crops, mills, and farms, depriving the Confederacy of much-needed food supplies. To the east, Sherman marched from Atlanta to Savannah, destroying everything of military value in his path. He then turned north, burned Columbia, South Carolina, and moved into North Carolina, leaving devastation in his wake.

The death knell of the Confederacy sounded April 2, 1865, when Lee was forced to abandon Richmond and Petersburg. He attempted to retreat west, but was cut off by Sheridan's cavalry at Appomattox on April 8.

The use of Union military power was the key to the liberty long awaited by the southern slave population. Freedom from bondage was obtained, but the tremendous cost in lives, so common in a civil war, was shared by both the North and the South.

Map References

The exercises and questions in this chapter relate to the text of Chapter 16 of *Liberty, Equality, Power: A History of the American People* and the following maps.

Principal Military Campaigns of the Civil War (p. 515)

Peninsula Campaign, April-May 1862 (p. 535)

Map Exercises

1. Locate with a dot and label the following cities on Map 16:
   a. Harpers Ferry
   b. Washington, D.C.
   c. Vicksburg
   d. Jackson (MS)
   e. Memphis
   f. Nashville
   g. Richmond
   h. Chattanooga
   i. Atlanta
   j. Andersonville
   k. Savannah
   l. Wilmington (NC)
   m. Charleston
   n. Appomattox
   o. Knoxville

2. Locate and label the following rivers on Map 16:
   a. Rappahannock
   b. Yazoo
   c. Chattahoochee
   d. Cape Fear
   e. James

3. Locate and give the dates of the following battles on Map 16:
   a. Stones River
   b. Antietam
   c. Chancellorsville
   d. Gettysburg
   e. Chickamauga

Map 16: Civil War, 1862–1865

Relating Maps and Text

1. In May 1861 Union General Benjamin Butler refused to return three slaves who had fled to his lines near _____ at the mouth of the _____. Butler called these escapees _____, a term that stuck.

2. In early September 1862 Robert E. Lee led his troops across the _____ into _____, hoping another victory would break the North's will to fight and bring about diplomatic recognition of the Confederacy by _____ and _____.

3. The Battle of _____ resulted in the highest casualties of any single day in American history.

4. The Emancipation Proclamation of 1863 freed slaves in those southern states still in rebellion. It exempted the _____ states, _____, and the parts of _____ and _____ already occupied by the Union.

5. In the fall of 1862 "Peace Democrats" in the northern states of _____ and _____ called for an armistice and peace talks with the Confederacy.

6. The worst draft riots in the North occurred in _____ in July 1863.

7. The Pacific Railroad Act made land grants and loans available to railroad companies to encourage the building of a transcontinental railroad from _____ to _____.

8. Union victories at _____ in November 1863 demoralized the Confederacy and led to the promotion of _____ to the position of general-in-chief of the Union armies.

9. In 1862, Union commanders in the occupied regions of the states of _____, _____, and _____ began to organize black regiments.

10. The 54th Massachusetts Infantry, the first black regiment raised in the North, led the attack on _____, part of the Confederate defenses of the city of _____.

11. After direct assaults failed in June 1864, U. S. Grant began a siege of the cities of _____ and _____ that would last more than nine months.

12. William T. Sherman's capture of _____ and Philip Sheridan's victories in the _____ Valley ensured Lincoln's reelection in 1864.

Essay Questions

1. Why did the Emancipation Proclamation exempt slavery in the border states?
2. Why was Vicksburg such an important city to the defense of the Confederacy?

Chapter 17
Reconstruction, 1863–1877

Chapter Summary

After four long years of fighting, the Civil War ended in 1865. The coming of peace, however, did not restore unity. Twelve years would pass before the states enjoyed a semblance of unity. That period of political rebuilding was known as Reconstruction, a process that actually began during the Civil War. In accordance with Abraham Lincoln's 1863 Proclamation of Amnesty, Louisiana, Arkansas, and Tennessee were "reconstructed." However, Congress refused to recognize the new governments of these southern states.

After the assassination of Lincoln, Andrew Johnson became president. During his administration, the allegedly reconstructed southern states of South Carolina and Mississippi enacted legislation, the Black Codes, that compromised the freedom of the former slave population. Race riots in New Orleans and Memphis in 1866 convinced many northerners that only the use of federal military power could guarantee the liberty and equality of blacks in the former Confederacy.

The Republican Congress therefore passed the Reconstruction Acts of 1867. These acts divided the ten southern states into five military districts. Then the Congress proposed the Fourteenth Amendment. This powerful amendment guaranteed blacks citizenship and forbade a state from depriving a citizen of "life, liberty, or property" without due process of law.

It was clear by 1867 that the executive and legislative branches of the federal government were engaged in a power struggle. When Congress passed the Tenure of Office Act, Johnson challenged its authority to infringe upon his executive power by violating the law. Subsequently, Congress impeached the president. Even though the attempt to convict him of the charges failed, Johnson's authority as decision maker disappeared.

By 1870, all of the southern states had completed the Reconstruction process, which included ratifying not only the Fourteenth Amendment but also the Fifteenth. Under the power of the federal government, this equal suffrage amendment mandated that a state could not deny a citizen the right to vote because of race.

During the latter part of the 1860s, the nation witnessed the rise of racism in the South. The Ku Klux Klan became active in Louisiana, Georgia, Arkansas, and Tennessee. This antiminority organization intimidated black voters with violence in the 1868 election. However, the Republican candidate, Ulysses S. Grant, still won the election. Later, in Colfax, Louisiana, armed whites and black militia engaged in a bloody battle that saw almost one hundred militia killed. As a result of the Klan's intimidation tactics and violence, Congress passed the Ku Klux Klan Act in 1871. This legislation was designed to suppress terrorist societies by invoking presidential power to send in federal troops to preserve order.

Meanwhile, the Grant administration also had to deal with foreign issues and domestic economic woes. Negotiations with Great Britain were jeopardized by Fenian raids into Canada, which occurred three times from 1866 to 1871. However, United States military power finally halted the raids, and the Treaty of Washington was signed in 1871. This treaty resolved the "Alabama Claims" with Great Britain, and tensions soon eased.

The collapse of the Northern Pacific Railroad in 1873 triggered a sharp depression as hundreds of banks and other businesses failed. The United States would not emerge from hard times resulting from the Panic of 1873 for five years.

By 1875, only South Carolina, Florida, Louisiana, and Mississippi remained under Republican control, and many northerners were disillusioned with the militarily enforced governments in those southern states. The disputed election of 1876 and the political compromise that broke the electoral deadlock between the Republican Rutherford B. Hayes and the Democrat Samuel Tilden solved the problem of federally enforced military governments in the South. However, the compromise assured the return of white Democrats to political power at the expense of black voter equality.

Map References

The exercises and questions in this chapter relate to the following maps and corresponding text in Chapter 17 of *Liberty, Equality, Power: A History of the American People.*

> Black and White Participation in Constitutional Conventions, 1867–1868 (p. 597)
>
> Reconstruction in the South (p. 600)
>
> Hayes–Tilden Disputed Election of 1876 (p. 609)

Map Exercises

1. Locate and label the following on Map 17:
    a. Louisiana
    b. South Carolina
    c. Mississippi
    d. Arkansas
    e. Tennessee
    f. Texas
    g. Georgia
    h. Florida
    i. Ohio
    j. Virginia
    k. Kentucky
    l. New York
    m. Utah Territory
    n. Pennsylvania
    o. Oregon

Relating Maps and Text

1. The first Confederate state to reorganize its government under President Lincoln's 10 percent plan in 1864 was _____. The states of _____ and _____ soon followed.

2. When Congress seized control of Reconstruction, only the state of _____ had been readmitted to the Union.

3. Under the Reconstruction Acts of 1867, the fifth military district included the states of _____ and _____. Only the state of _____ was not combined with another state in a military district.

Map 17: The United States in the 1870s

4. Black Codes, state laws intended to restrict the civil rights of freedpeople, were especially discriminatory in _____ and _____ .

5. In the state constitutional conventions held in the South in the winter and spring of 1867 and 1868, blacks were in the majority as delegates in only the _____ convention. In all other states except _____ , white delegates were in the majority.

6. On several occasions from 1866 to 1871, small armies of Irish-American Union Army veterans known as _____ launched raids into _____ .

7. In an effort to control the Ku Klux Klan during Reconstruction, President Grant suspended the writ of habeas corpus in several counties in _____ .

8. The Union Pacific and _____ railroads were joined at _____ in 1869. The Northern Pacific Railroad was to build west from _____ .

Harcourt Brace & Company

9. By 1875, the four southern states that still remained under the control of the Republican Party were _____, _____, _____, and _____.

10. The _____ in 1871 established arbitration procedures that resulted in the United States's winning damage claims against _____, thus settling the long-standing _____.

11. In the presidential election of 1876, electoral votes from the states of _____, _____, _____, and _____ were in dispute.

Essay Questions

1. To what extent did freedpeople enjoy liberty and power after the Civil War?

2. How was the disputed presidential election of 1876 resolved? What groups and individuals gained power as a result of the settlement? What groups and individuals lost power?

Answer Key

Chapter 1

Map Exercises

Map 1-A: North America and the Caribbean

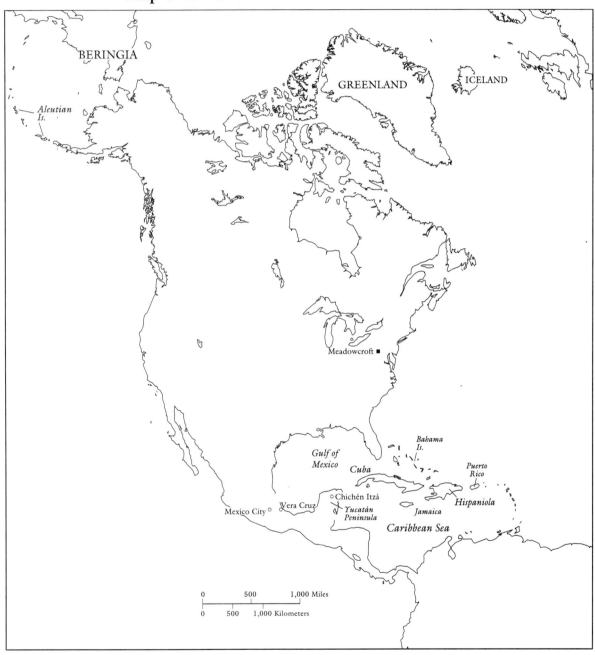

Map 1-B: Africa and the Mediterranean in the 15th Century

Relating Maps and Text

1. Beringia
2. Central America
    Mexico
3. Erik the Red
    Greenland
    Leif
    Vinland
    wood
4. Madeira
    Azores
    Cape Verde
    Bartolomeu Dias
    Vasco da Gama

5. Canary Islands
    Aragon
    Castile
6. a. Juan Ponce de León
    b. Vasco Núñez de Balboa
    c. Ferdinand Magellan
    d. Hernán Cortés
    e. Francisco Pizarro
    f. Francisco Vasquez de Coronado
7. Cahokia
    Hohokam
    Anasazi
8. 50

Essay Question

1. By 1492, European nations were creating modern nation-states and were competing for resources to pay for armies that seemed increasingly necessary. Trade, especially with Asia, provided some of the required wealth. Portugal proved that conquest and colonization could be a profitable addition to a trading system when the Portuguese seized control of parts of the African coastline.

    When Europeans came in contact with Americans, they faced cultures that had entirely different religious beliefs, warfare practices, and cultural norms (including ideas about gender and the ownership of property). Misunderstandings contributed to conflict. Moreover, some of the American peoples had gold and inferior weapons—too tempting a combination for the Europeans, particularly the Spanish, to resist. In short, it was more profitable for the Spanish to defeat the American peoples than to coexist with them. Of the Native Americans not killed in armed conflict or, more likely, by European diseases, many were enslaved.

Chapter 2

Map Exercises

Map 2: Atlantic Coast of North America

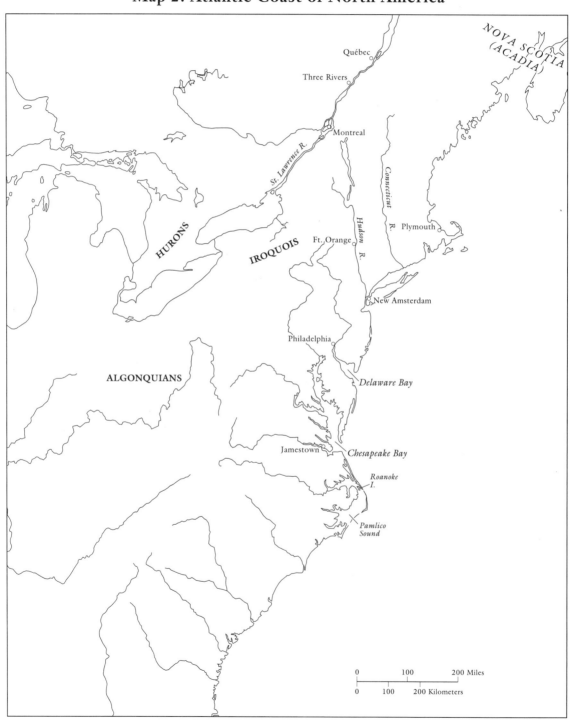

Relating Maps and Text

1. a. Carolinas
        Nova Scotia
        Manhattan Island
    b. St. Lawrence
    c. Acadia (Nova Scotia)
        Québec
2. Manhattan
    New Amsterdam
    Fort Orange
    Iroquois
3. a. Giovanni Cabato (John Cabot)
        Newfoundland
    b. Francis Drake
        circumnavigation
    c. Roanoke Island
        Walter Ralegh
4. London Company
    Jamestown
    John Smith
    John Rolfe
        tobacco
5. Maryland
6. sugar
7. Pilgrims
    Puritans
    food
    lumber
8. Roger Williams
    Anne Hutchinson
    Connecticut
9. rice
    slavery
10. New Netherland
    New York
    New York
    New Orange
11. West New Jersey
    Pennsylvania
    wheat
    flour

Essay Question

1. The Spanish, after decimating the Indian population in the Caribbean islands in the early
    1500s, established missions in Florida and New Mexico and converted, rather than enslaved, the
    Indians. The French established Jesuit missions in the area of the Great Lakes and traded with
    the Indians for furs. The Dutch in the 1620s established a fur trading post at Fort Orange on the
    Hudson River and attempted peaceful relations with the Indians of the area. The English were
    farmers who cut down trees, took the land as their own, and antagonized the Indians. Warfare
    between the Indians and English became common.

Chapter 3

Map Exercises

Map 3: British Colonies, circa 1720

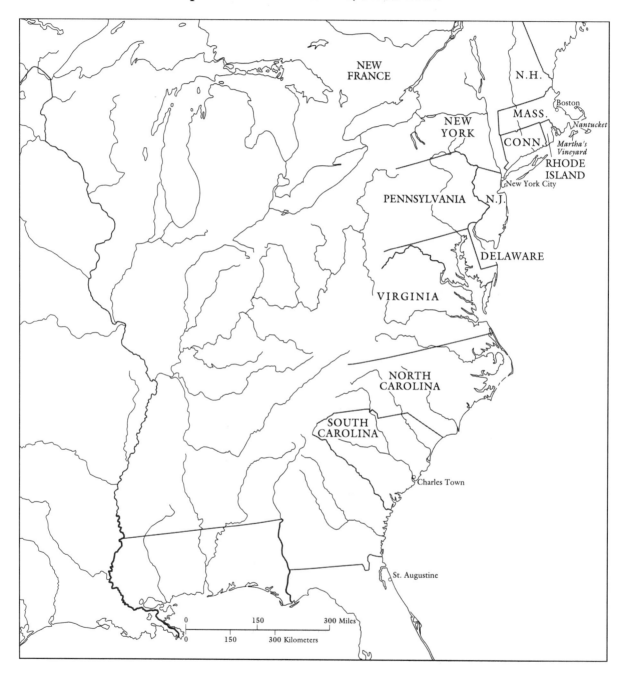

Relating Maps and Text

1. Dutch
   West Indian
   Chesapeake
   Amsterdam
   Navigation Acts
2. Martha's Vineyard
   Natick
3. Occaneechee
   Pamunkey
   Bacon's
   Jamestown
4. Edmund Andros
   Dominion of New England

   Massachusetts
   New Hampshire
   Plymouth
   Rhode Island
   Connecticut
   New York
5. England
   Scotland
   Great Britain
6. Taos Pueblo
   New Mexico
7. middle ground
   New France

Essay Question

1. The city of Philadelphia became a prosperous port city as an exporter of wheat and flour to other British colonies, especially the Caribbean. New York merchants had access to docking facilities just as in New York, but operated under an elected government as opposed to the Duke of York's absolutist government with arbitrary taxation.

Chapter 4

Map Exercises

Map 4: Northeast during the French and Indian War

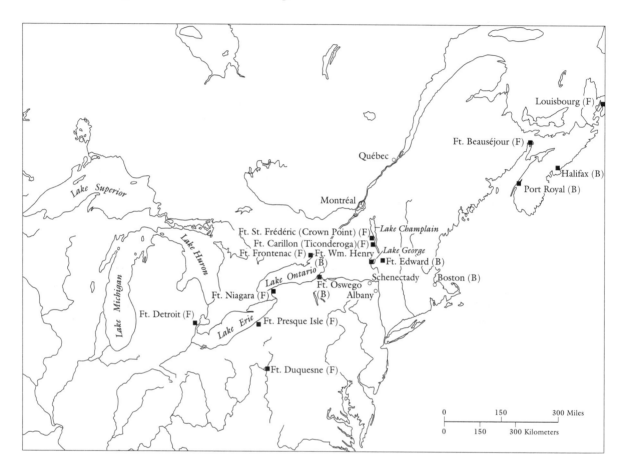

Relating Maps and Text

1. Chesapeake
   gangs
   10
   Wheat
   Norfolk
   Baltimore
   shipbuilding
2. South Carolina
   task
   indigo
   textile
3. Pennsylvania
   Philadelphia
   New England
4. Massachusetts
5. Boston
   New York Weekly Journal
6. Georgia
   Savannah
   silk

   wine
   slaves
   hard liquor
7. Congregational
   middle
   Britain
8. Florida
   Gracia Real de Santa Teresa de Mose (or Mose)
9. Presque Isle
   Duquesne
   Alleghenies
10. Pennsylvania
11. France
    Austria
    Russia
    Prussia
    Britain
    Spain

Essay Question

1. Some developments advancing equality included opportunities afforded by the availability of new land (taken from Indians); the Great Awakening, which increased the participation of women and non-elites in religion; and a widely shared franchise, which allowed nearly three-fourths of adult white males to vote in the colonies.

   Inequality was demonstrated by the anglicization and social stratification of American society (fashion, houses, newspapers, professions); the growth of slavery, which not only denied that people of African descent were equal to those of European descent, but also created growing differences in wealth between white planters and other whites and growing differences between slaves in different regions of the country; the treatment of Indians, who were sometimes regarded as less than human; changes in politics or public life, which came increasingly under the control of gentlemen property holders; the Enlightenment, which differentiated between elite, educated professionals (ministers, doctors, lawyers) and the rest of the people; and differential treatment of American and British officers in the military.

Chapter 5

Map Exercises

Map 5: Late Colonial America

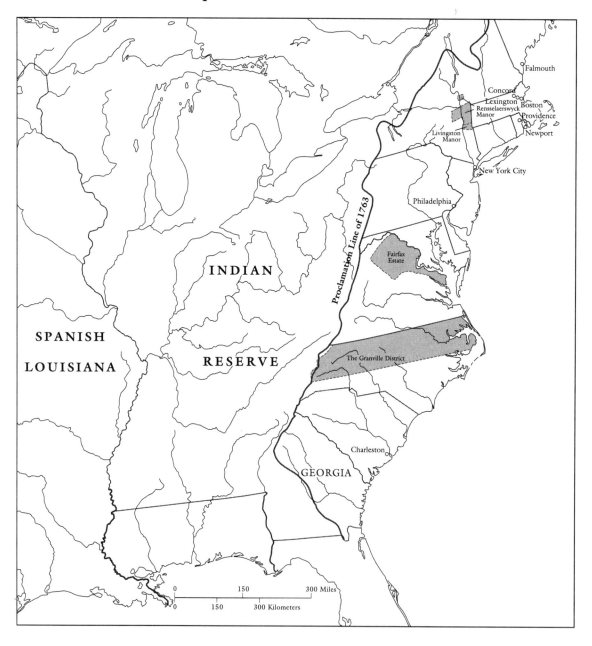

Relating Maps and Text

1. Guadeloupe
   Martinique
   Canada
2. Proclamation of 1763
   Appalachian
3. Pontiac's War
   Paxton Boys
4. New York City
   Georgia
   Boston
   Newport (RI)

5. New York
   New York Restraining Act
6. Providence
7. Boston
   Massachusetts
   New England
8. Salem
   Concord
9. Staten Island

Essay Question

1. The British wanted the colonies to pay a portion of the costs for defense, since after the French and Indian War the size of British North America increased tremendously. To raise revenues, Parliament passed tax legislation such as the Stamp Act of 1765 and the Townshend Revenue Act of 1767 (an import tax on tea, paper, glass, and red and white lead) without the consent of the colonial legislatures. In addition, the British army began withdrawing from frontier forts and moving men and supplies to the coastal cities, thus threatening the liberty of the colonials.

   Vice-admiralty courts were given appellate jurisdiction in Boston, Philadelphia, and Charleston, and the Quartering Act was invoked. On March 5, 1770, the Boston Massacre occurred, an incident that saw several colonists killed and the public even more convinced that Parliament meant to deprive the colonies of their traditional liberties.

Harcourt Brace & Company

Chapter 6

Map Exercises

Map 6-A: Revolutionary War in the Northern States

Map 6-B: Virginia and the Yorktown Campaign

Relating Maps and Text

1. Newport, Rhode Island
   Long Island
2. Saratoga
3. Gibraltar
   British West Florida
   East Florida
4. Virginia
   Massachusetts
5. Deep South
   Charleston
   King's Mountain
6. Pennsylvania
   New Jersey

7. Virginia
   Yorktown
8. Pennsylvania
   Philadelphia
9. six
   36
   640
10. Philadelphia
    Rhode Island
    Connecticut
    Virginia
    New Jersey

Essay Question

1. Under the Treaty of Paris, the United States roughly doubled in size as it took possession of the land west of the Appalachians to the Mississippi and north of Florida, which Spain regained. For the new United States, the western lands became a significant social and political issue. Settlers coveted the rich farmland, states squabbled over possession of the region, and Indians fought hard to keep white settlers from moving in and seizing control. After states ceded authority over western lands to the federal government, the Land Ordinance of 1785 and the Northwest Ordinance of 1787 established policies for surveying, selling, settling, and governing the region.

   The war also contributed to the further development of sectionalism in the colonies/states. The need for revenue to pay war debts led to clashes such as Shays's Rebellion between the courts, generally considered to represent the urban merchants along the coast, and farmers in the interior. Likewise, the debates over state constitutions and bills of rights resulted in clashes between the interior and the coastal regions. Finally, the war contributed to regional changes in slavery. In the North, Pennsylvania issued the first gradual emancipation statute in 1780, and the other northern states followed suit by 1804, when New Jersey became the last to enact legislation. In the South, however, emancipation was strongly resisted by planters, especially after the 1790s, when cotton became increasingly important as a cash crop.

Chapter 7

Map Exercises

Map 7: The West, circa 1800

Relating Maps and Text

1. New England
   South
   West
   "changing system"

2. Cherokee
   Creek
   Choctaw
   Chickasaw
   Seminole

3. Georgia
   "task system"
   "private fields"
   five

4. New York City

5. New England
   Pennsylvania
   Chesapeake

6. Vermont
   Rhode Island

7. Episcopal
   Congregational
   Baptist
   Methodist
   Presbyterian

Essay Question

1. After 1790 the soil of the Chesapeake (Maryland, Delaware, and Virginia) was depleted by many years of tobacco farming. Farmers began moving out of the area and into Kentucky, Tennessee, and western Virginia. The planters who stayed switched crop production from slave-cultivated tobacco to grain and livestock, products that did not require as much slave labor. Farmers in Maryland and Delaware began freeing their slaves. After 1810 slaves in Virginia were sold in large numbers to planters cultivating the fertile cotton lands of Georgia, Alabama, and Mississippi.

Chapter 8

Map Exercises

Map 8-A: United States, circa 1804

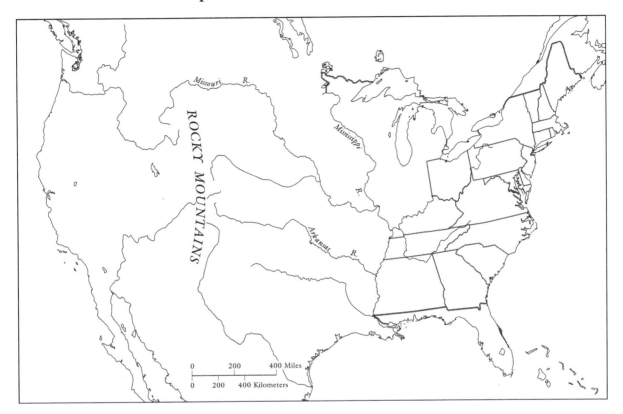

Map 8-B: War of 1812

Relating Maps and Text

1. New York City
   Potomac
2. South Carolina
   Northeast
3. Austria
   Prussia
   Britain
4. Pinckney's
   Mississippi River
   New Orleans
5. Pennsylvania
   New York
   South Carolina
6. New Orleans

   Louisiana Territory
7. South
   West
   Kentucky
   South Carolina
   Georgia
8. Canada
   York (Toronto)
   Montreal
9. Tecumseh
   Thames River
10. Washington, D.C.
    Baltimore
11. Ghent

Essay Questions

1. The southern part of the Louisiana Purchase, because of its climate and rich, alluvial soils, seemed destined to become an agricultural region open to slavery. Northeasterners also feared that the farm states that would be carved from Upper Louisiana would support the Democratic Party, not the Federalist. Finally, northeasterners worried about losing power in Congress. If a large number of states were carved out of the Louisiana Purchase, older states in the Northeast would lose power in the Senate; if, as expected, the population grew quickly in the region, older states with stable or declining populations would steadily lose representation in the House.

2. The Northeast recognized that if a war broke out with England, coastal cities, shipping, and manufacturing would be vulnerable to attacks by the British navy. In addition, British from Canada could easily invade northeastern cities.

Chapter 9

Map Exercises

Map 9: United States during the Market Revolution

Relating Maps and Text

1. Philadelphia
   McCulloch v. *Maryland*
2. Ohio-Mississippi River
   steamboat
3. Erie Canal
   Albany
   Buffalo
   Syracuse
   Rochester
   Buffalo
4. Northeast
   Mid-Atlantic

Old Northwest
South
5. beef
   massive deforestation
6. ready-made clothes
   cloth
   labor
7. 82
   70
   40
   84

Essay Questions

1. The South had natural navigable waterways that could be used to transport crops to market. The Old Northwest also had rivers, but they generally ran north to south, and farmers and manufacturers needed to move goods from south to north and from west to east. After a high initial cost, canals made such transportation possible and extremely cheap.
2. Since the seventeenth century, the South had been an area of agricultural production. After 1815, the region grew slave-cultivated cotton for Northern and European textile markets. The production of a raw product, not finished, factory-produced consumer goods, was the emphasis in southern agriculture.

Chapter 10

Relating Geography and Text

1. New England
2. Rochester
3. Brooklyn
   Rochester
4. Hudson

   Catskills

   White

   Niagara Falls

5. Charleston, South Carolina

   Southampton County, Virginia

Essay Questions

1. Improved transportation (rail, steamboat, canal) brought Americans to nature and prompted a new consideration of the "contest" between nature and civilization in both art and literature. For the first time in U.S. history, people traveled to view scenery. People came to view nature as the sublime handiwork of God rather than a dark, forbidding, demon-filled place, as it had seemed to be in earlier times.

   Transportation also brought theater to rural audiences and vice versa: traveling troupes came to the countryside, and country folks traveled to cities to attend the theater. Theater became more democratized, more rowdy, sometimes even violent. The democratization of theater also meant its homogenization: minstrel shows, for example, followed a set formula that virtually everyone knew. Finally, theater, through the minstrel shows in particular, influenced cultural perceptions of African Americans, who were portrayed in the shows as humorous, musical, and highly sexual persons.

2. The founders of Mount Auburn Cemetery wanted it to be a place of learning in which nature could be experienced firsthand and people could face the cycle of life and death.

   Internet sites indicate that Mount Auburn still serves those purposes. It has become a favorite venue for birdwatchers (see the Virtual Birder® Web site at http://vbirder.iserver.net/vbirder/onLoc/onLocDirs/BOSSPR/). The cemetery is also frequently visited by school classes and other groups (see the site of the Friends of Mount Auburn Cemetery at http://vbirder.iserver.net/vbirder/onLoc/onLocDirs/BOSSPR/bg/mtauburn/Friends.html). The trees, flowers, and other plants attract many visitors. The cemetery features about 2,500 trees (over 350 varieties) and thousands of other plants (see the Michigan State University Extension Home Page at http://www.msue.msu.edu/son/mod70/70000106.html). [URLs accessed June 1998.]

Chapter 11

Map Exercises

Map 11: United States, circa 1840

Relating Maps and Text

1. Whig
   Democratic
2. South Carolina
   Georgia
   Tennessee
   Kentucky
   Arkansas
   New York
3. Massachusetts
   Connecticut
   Ohio
4. Pittsburgh
   Philadelphia
   New York
5. Massachusetts
   Maine
6. Philadelphia
7. American Colonization Society
   Liberia
   Great Britain
   The Liberator
   southern New England
   western New York
   northern Ohio
8. Oneida
9. Seneca Falls
   political

Essay Question

1. In the North the Whig Party was more politically influential than in the South. Whigs such as Horace Mann from Massachusetts favored centralized school systems that taught morality and built character. The North was also the region into which most immigrants moved. Schools were intended to serve as "Americanizing" institutions for immigrants, teaching them to value democratic republicanism, capitalism, and Protestantism, among other things. Immigrants were not always amenable to such influences.

   Southern schools were usually locally controlled, with a limited curriculum and a shorter school year. Members of the Democratic Party, who controlled the South, regarded mandatory schooling as an example of excessive government intervention into the patriarchal, independent, household establishment. With fewer immigrants (and virtually all of the nation's slaves) schooling seemed less necessary for Americanization purposes in the South.

Chapter 12

Map Exercises

Map 12: United States, circa 1848

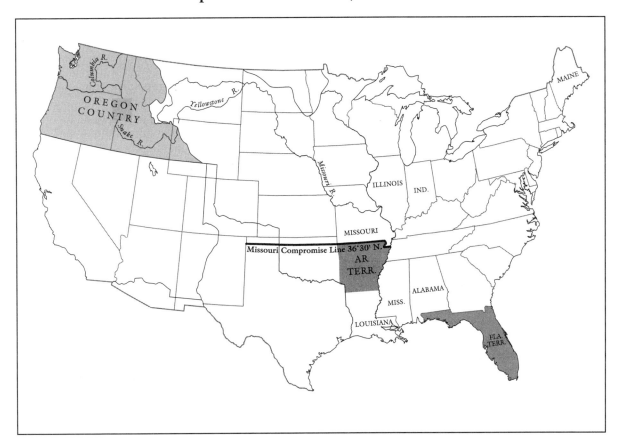

Relating Maps and Text

1. Massachusetts
   Maine
   Missouri
   36°30′
2. Mexico
   Peru
   Europe
   credit
   banknotes
3. Tennessee
   New Orleans
   Spanish Florida

4. New England
   South
   West
5. Rocky Mountains
   Florida
   Northwest Pacific Coast
6. Latin American republics
   European
   British
7. Georgia
8. South Carolina
9. seaport

Essay Question

1. In the 1830s, Jackson supported an Indian removal policy, even though the Marshall Court had declared that the state of Georgia had no claims to Cherokee land.

   In the Nullification Crisis in 1832, Jackson denied the alleged right, under the pretext of liberty, of South Carolina to nullify the Tariffs of 1828 and 1832. Jackson asked Congress for a Force Bill that would allow him to lead a federal army into South Carolina.

   Jackson vetoed a Congressional bill in 1832 that would have rechartered the National Bank. After his reelection in 1832, he began withdrawing federal funds from the National Bank and depositing them in state banks. These two bank-related episodes caused his political enemies to unite against Jackson in the new Whig Party formed in 1834. (Jackson's veto of the Maysville Road project and his "Specie Circular" may also be given as examples of his use of presidential powers.)

Harcourt Brace & Company

Chapter 13

Map Exercises

Map 13: Western United States in the 1840s

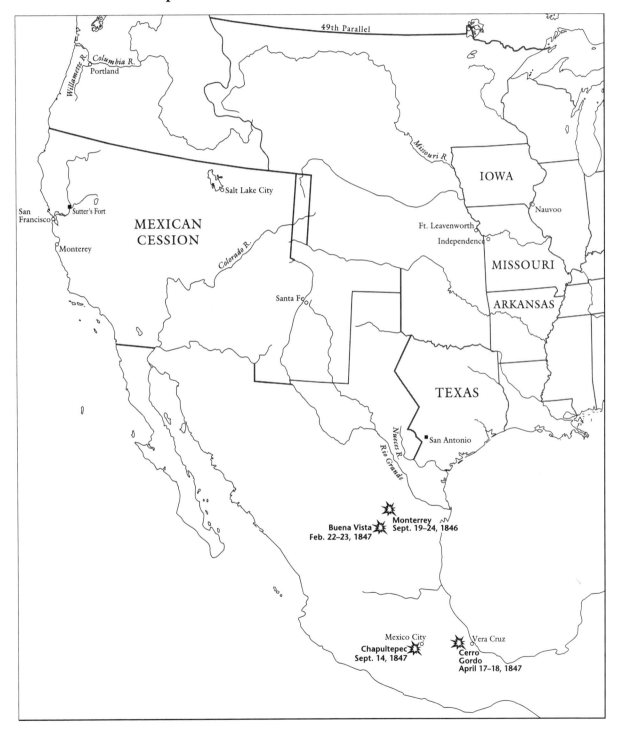

Relating Maps and Text

1. 95th meridian
2. Louisiana
   Missouri
   Arkansas
   Florida
   Texas
   Iowa
   Alabama
   Mississippi
   Iowa
3. Willamette
4. Santa Fe
   Sutter's Fort
5. Brigham Young
6. 30,000

   eastern
   San Jacinto River
   President Antonio López de Santa Anna
7. Texas
   Oregon
8. Santa Fe
   Chihuahua
   Monterrey
   Buena Vista
9. Vera Cruz
   Mexico City
10. California
11. Cuba
    Nicaragua

Essay Questions

1. By gaining title to the waters of Puget Sound south of Vancouver Island, the United States developed a naval base there and evolved into a Pacific Ocean naval power. The formalization of the boundary with British Canada allowed the United States to concentrate military forces at posts south of that border and suppress the Indian tribes that opposed white settlement.

2. The Compromise of 1850 did, in fact, offer something for both North and South. California was admitted into the Union as a free state. The New Mexico and Utah territories were organized with no restrictions against slavery, despite Utah's being above the Missouri Compromise line. The Texas-New Mexico border dispute was settled in favor of New Mexico, and Texas was paid $10 million as compensation. The slave trade was abolished in the District of Columbia, but the institution of slavery was guaranteed there. The passage of the Fugitive Slave Act made it more difficult for runaway slaves to keep their new-found liberty.

   Both North and South thought they had given up more than they gained in the arrangement, which probably indicates that the compromise could not have gone more one way or another to favor either side. Northerners disliked the popular sovereignty provision, which effectively revoked the Missouri Compromise line and opened up the central and northern territories to slavery. Also unpopular in the North was the Fugitive Slave Law, which seemed an unconstitutional extension of federal power. Southerners disliked the popular sovereignty provision of the compromise because it was a step back from absolute property rights. They also complained, with reason, that the North did not vigorously enforce the Fugitive Slave Law.

Harcourt Brace & Company

Chapter 14

Map Exercises

Map 14: United States, circa 1856

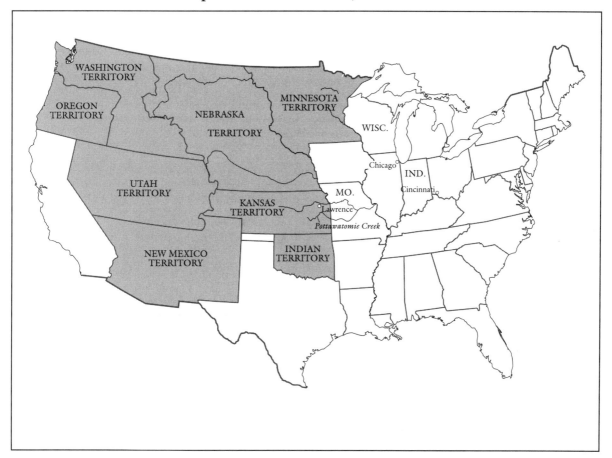

Relating Maps and Text

1. Kansas-Nebraska Bill
   Kansas
2. "Know Nothings"
   Northeast
   border states
3. Missouri
   Kansas
   Missouri
   Arkansas
   Texas
4. Illinois
   Wisconsin Territory
   Missouri
5. Old Northwest
   Northeast

Chicago
6. New England
7. doubled
   three fifths
8. five
   Forty
   manufacturing
   commercial
   equaled
9. Cuba
10. wages
    opportunities
11. Harpers Ferry
    Appalachian Mountains

Essay Questions

1. The climate of the area immediately west of Missouri seemed suitable for a slave-based agricultural economy. Slaveholders in Missouri were anxious to move west into the area and acquire new farmland. In addition, if slavery was prohibited in Nebraska, as it might be unless the 36°30' prohibition under the Missouri Compromise of 1820 was repealed, it would put the state in the unenviable position of being surrounded on three sides by free territory. That situation could have made it easier for slaves in Missouri to escape.

2. Both sections had economic power: the North was the manufacturing and commercial center of the nation and had a diverse system of agriculture as well. The South's economy, while strong, was based largely on one product, cotton, and a labor system, slavery, that was becoming less and less stable. The South weathered the 1857 depression much more easily than did the North.

   Both sections had what might be called "moral" power: the North was becoming increasingly antislavery, which seemed to be a position more in keeping with Northerners' view of Protestant Christianity, upon which all moral issues were decided in that era. Southerners pointed to the immorality of northern "wage slavery" and described the South's system favorably: slaves were cared for even when they were sick or injured or old; in the North, sick, injured, or old workers were not paid and were not otherwise provided for.

   Both sections had political power: the North, with its growing population, was gaining control of the House of Representatives and the electoral college. The elections of 1856 and 1860 sharply demonstrated the imbalance of power in the electoral college. The South dominated the Supreme Court and at least held its own in the Senate.

   Finally, both sides had the power of tradition and the Founders. The northern antislavery position seemed to mesh with the Declaration of Independence and its statement that "all men are created equal" and that all have the right to liberty. The South had the Constitution, with its protection of property and allusions to slavery, on its side. In addition, southerners pointed out that such revered leaders as George Washington and Thomas Jefferson had been slaveholders.

Harcourt Brace & Company

Chapter 15

Map Exercises

Map 15: Civil War, 1860–1862

Relating Maps and Text

1. Pennsylvania
    Illinois
    Indiana
2. South Carolina
    Mississippi
    Florida
3. Delaware
    Maryland
    Kentucky
    Missouri
    West Virginia

4. Missouri
5. Confederacy
6. Great Britain
7. west
    east
    Richmond
8. Henry
    Tennessee
    Donelson
    Nashville

Essay Question

1. The 3,500 miles of southern coastline, with its inlets, harbors, bays and river systems, provided natural havens for Confederate blockade runners to anchor and wait for the thin line of Union ships to shift to other locations. The Union did not have enough blockade vessels the first year of the war to effectively seal off all southern ports. Rivers with several channels to the sea, for example, the Mississippi, were particularly difficult to obstruct completely.

    The South's cotton embargo attempted to create a cotton shortage in Great Britain in an effort to compel English military intervention on behalf of the Confederacy. However, a cotton surplus in England from bumper crops in 1859 and 1860 spoiled the South's efforts.

Chapter 16

Map Exercises

Map 16: Civil War, 1862–1865

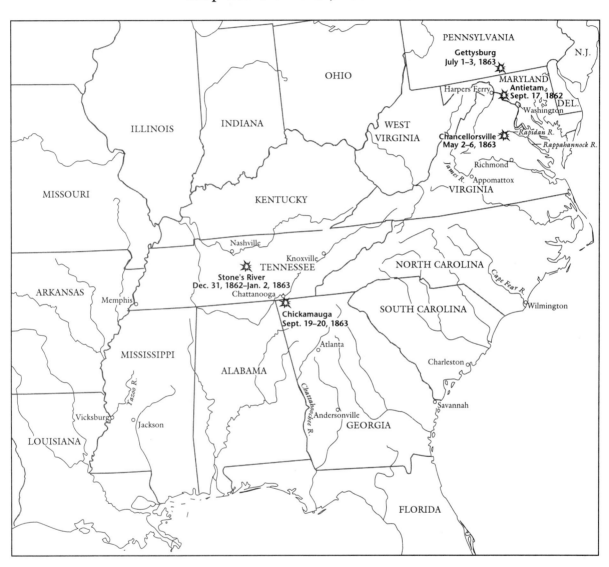

Relating Maps and Text

1. Fortress Monroe
   James River
   "contraband of war"
2. Potomac River
   Maryland
   Great Britain
   France
3. Antietam
4. border
   Tennessee
   Louisiana
   Virginia
5. Illinois
   Indiana
6. New York City
7. Omaha
   Sacramento
8. Chattanooga
   U. S. Grant
9. Louisiana
   South Carolina
   Missouri
10. Fort Wagner
    Charleston
11. Petersburg
    Richmond
12. Atlanta
    Shenandoah

Essay Questions

1. Unionists in the border states might have rebelled if the slaves were freed. Also, enemy property could be confiscated if it was being used for military purposes, and Lincoln presented the Emancipation Proclamation as a military necessity. Border slaves, though considered property, did not belong to the enemy, since the border states were not Confederate territory.

2. Vicksburg controlled Union naval movements on the Mississippi River. If Vicksburg could be seized, the Confederacy would not be able to move troops and supplies from Texas, Arkansas, and western Louisiana to the eastern theater of the war. Gaining control of the Mississippi and cutting the Confederacy in half was part of the Union's "Anaconda Plan."

Harcourt Brace & Company

Chapter 17

Map Exercises

Map 17: The United States in the 1870s

Relating Maps and Text

1. Louisiana
   Arkansas
   Tennessee
2. Tennessee
3. Louisiana
   Texas
   Virginia
4. South Carolina
   Mississippi
5. South Carolina
   Louisiana
6. Fenians
   Canada
7. South Carolina

8. Central Pacific
   Promontory Point, Utah Territory
   Duluth, Minnesota
9. South Carolina
   Florida
   Mississippi
   Louisiana
10. Treaty of Washington
    Great Britain
    Alabama Claims
11. Louisiana
    South Carolina
    Florida
    Oregon

Essay Questions

1. Freedpeople's liberty and power were sharply limited after the Civil War. State and local Black Codes restricted their civil rights and economic opportunities. Although the Fourteenth and Fifteenth Amendments guaranteed adult black males the right to vote, states often found ways to discourage or prevent freedmen's exercising of the franchise. The Freedmen's Bureau provided some protection and educational opportunities, but freedpeople fell victim to groups such as the Ku Klux Klan. When the U.S. Army was pulled out of the South in 1877, freedpeople's position in southern society was not much different than it had been under slavery.

2. To determine whether the Republican, Rutherford B. Hayes, or the Democrat, Samuel Tilden, should receive the disputed electoral votes, Congress appointed a special fifteen-member electoral commission that was composed of five senators, five representatives, and five justices of the Supreme Court. Seven commissioners were Democrats, seven were Republicans, and one was an independent. When the independent, a Supreme Court justice, was named to the Senate, he had to give up his position on the commission, and all of the remaining justices were Republicans. By a party-line vote of eight to seven, the commission determined that Hayes should receive the disputed votes. To stop a threatened filibuster in the Democrat-dominated House, Hayes or his representatives promised the South generous internal improvements, control of southern patronage, federal aid for a southern transcontinental railroad, and the withdrawal of federal troops from Louisiana and South Carolina. The compromise ended Reconstruction in the southern states.

   Because their candidate secured the presidency, Republicans gained political power at the national level. For the same reason, Hayes himself gained power. Southern Democrats gained power at the local and state level: the end of Reconstruction meant that they controlled southern politics and the southern economy. The compromise clearly cost Samuel Tilden power. More significantly, however, it cost the freedpeople. They lost the political and economic power that they had begun to build following the Civil War and would face increasing discrimination under the Jim Crow laws. Other losers of power included the carpetbaggers and scalawags of the South, who depended on the army, and the army and its generals. Under Congressional Reconstruction, the generals in each of the military districts had had almost unlimited discretionary power.